Eccentric
LONDON

Eccentric
LONDON

Tom Quinn • *Photography by* Ricky Leaver

NEW HOLLAND

First published in 2005 by New Holland Publishers (UK) Ltd
London • Cape Town • Sydney • Auckland

www.newhollandpublishers.com

Garfield House, 86–88 Edgware Road, London W2 2EA, United Kingdom

80 McKenzie Street, Cape Town 8001, South Africa

14 Aquatic Drive, Frenchs Forest, NSW 2086, Australia

218 Lake Road, Northcote, Auckland, New Zealand

10 9 8 7 6 5 4 3 2 1

ISBN 1 84330 896 7

Publishing Manager: Jo Hemmings
Senior Editor: Kate Michell
Assistant Editor: Rose Hudson
Cover Design and Design: Alan Marshall
Cartography: Bill Smuts
Indexer: Dorothy Frame
Production: Joan Woodroffe

Reproduction by Pica Digital Pte Ltd, Singapore
Printed and bound in Singapore by Kyodo Printing Co. (Singapore) Pte Ltd

Photographs appearing on the cover and prelim pages are as follows:
Front cover (clockwise from top left): Cleopatra's Needle; Dinosaurs in Crystal Palace;
Twinings Tea Shop; Highgate Cemetery; Lock & Co. Hatters; Japanese Peace Pagoda, Battersea Park.
Spine: Seven Dials, Covent Garden. Back cover: Saatchi Gallery. Front flap: Dr Johnson's House.
Back flap: The Savoy's black cat.
Page 1: John Donne's Monument, St Paul's Cathedral. Page 2: Highgate Cemetery.
Page 3: Saatchi Gallery, Albert Embankment. Opposite: Japanese Peace Pagoda, Battersea Park.
Page 6 (left) Brixton Windmill; (middle) G. Smith & Sons snuff shop, Shaftesbury Avenue;
(right) Japanese Peace Pagoda, Battersea Park. Page 7 (left): Prince Albert's statue, Holborn Circus;
(middle) Gordon's Wine Bar, Villiers Street; (right) Crystal Palace dinosaurs.
Page 8 (left): Apothecaries Hall, Cobham House, Blackfriars; (right) Narcissus Hall, Leighton House,
Holland Park Road, Kensington. Page 9 (left): Lock & Co. Hatters, St James's; (right) Crystal Palace
dinosaurs. Page 128: Twinings Tea Shop.

Contents

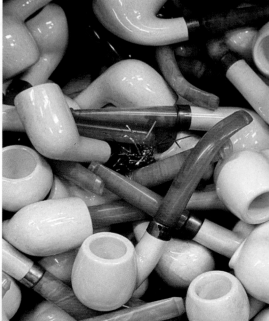

Introduction

If great age tends to bring eccentricity with it, then London is almost by definition an eccentric city. The ancient rules and systems of governance that have survived the centuries to baffle historians create numerous bizarre anomalies, and when these anomalies are combined with a city whose physical growth has been virtually piecemeal over two millennia it is not surprising that London is a mass of oddities.

London's eccentricity can also be attributed to our love of the old ways: dusty traditions, archaic rituals and ceremonies which continue to be practised despite, on the face of it, no longer being necessary. Black Rod hammering on the door of the House of Commons each day is a good example, or the pursuivants at the College of Arms initiating prosecutions against those who infringe the rules governing the use of gules, azure and archant. And just as we love the ceremonial past, so we love the physical past – the streets and squares, the warehouses and docks, the towers and cottages that have survived the centuries in a thousand different architectural styles.

The historic layers of London stretch so far back – to Roman times and beyond – that the past can seem almost tangible: modern buildings have ancient foundations or are built above tunnels, long-abandoned wells, Roman villas, medieval cesspits or vanished rivers. In the City proper, Victorian

BELOW: *A glimpse into the old metropolis through the City of London's Apothecaries Hall.*

BELOW RIGHT: *The extraordinary, sumptuous interior of Leighton House in Bayswater.*

warehouses and other buildings rest on the old Roman city walls, and beneath those walls lie earlier, Celtic structures.

And if much of the physical fabric of the ancient city survives, though usually hidden beneath the modern streets, much that is odd and ancient in London's social and business life also survives. There are snuff shops, tea sellers that have survived since Georgian times, 17th-century hatters and wine sellers, each operating out of premises unchanged over generations; there are bizarre little pet cemeteries, dinosaur parks and Victorian pumping stations designed to look like Moorish palaces.

And, of course, London contains, uniquely, two cities – an eccentric enough fact in itself. The City of Westminster and the City of London are each governed by very different rules. In the City of London, for example, an ancient ordinance defines a road as a highway without houses – which is why, to this day, no thoroughfare in the City may be called a road: it's either a street or an alley. In the City of Westminster eccentricities are equally well distributed: the Strand, for example, still refuses to adopt the universal system of listing its houses with odd numbers on one side and evens on the other; instead, houses are numbered one after another up one side of the street and then down the other. Or, take the short road to the entrance to the Savoy Hotel: bizarrely, this is the only road in the country that insists you drive on the wrong side!

And away from the physical eccentricity of London there is the vast history of London characters: oddballs and inventors, mavericks and madmen – men such as Stanley Green, who spent his life campaigning against protein-eating, or Walter Rothschild, who taught two pairs of zebras to pull his carriage down The Mall.

Whatever your interest – architecture, history or people – you will find much to enjoy in this guide to the peculiarities of what is one of the world's most endearingly eccentric cities.

BELOW LEFT: *Traditional headwear can still be purchased at Lock & Co. Hatters in St James's.*
BELOW: *This Victorian dinosaur is one of a number hidden away in a south London park.*

Soho to Westminster

Soho has always been a place of pleasure and scandal while, just a short distance away, Westminster looks along the river with a solemn, self-important air that speaks of government and the grand state occasion. The journey between these two very different places may be a short one – little more than a mile or two – yet it takes us on an odyssey through the odd and the quirky, the mad and the bad. Rich in history, the journey from Soho to Westminster is an expedition into the eccentric byways of one of the world's great capitals.

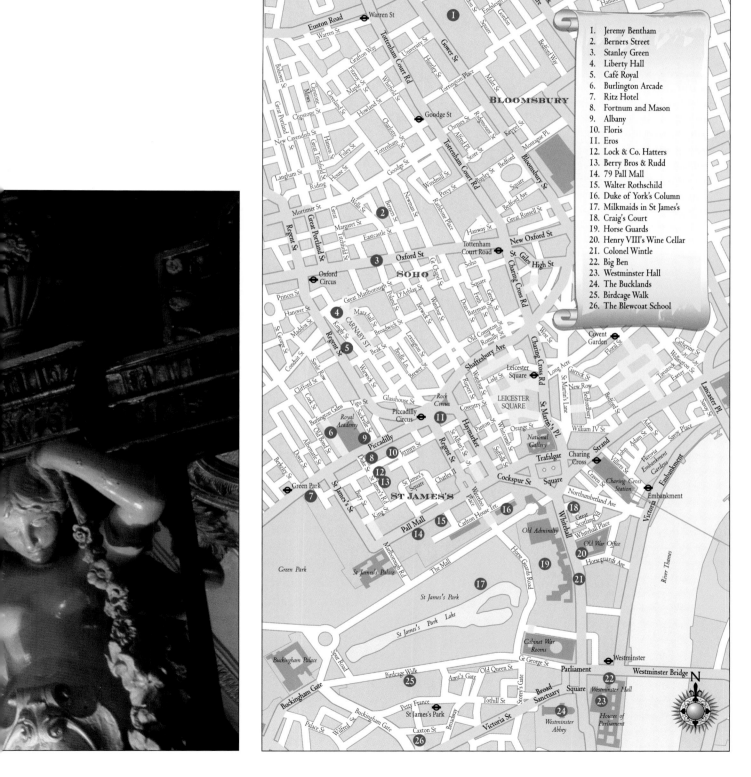

1. Jeremy Bentham
2. Berners Street
3. Stanley Green
4. Liberty Hall
5. Café Royal
6. Burlington Arcade
7. Ritz Hotel
8. Fortnum and Mason
9. Albany
10. Floris
11. Eros
12. Lock & Co. Hatters
13. Berry Bros & Rudd
14. 79 Pall Mall
15. Walter Rothschild
16. Duke of York's Column
17. Milkmaids in St James's
18. Craig's Court
19. Horse Guards
20. Henry VIII's Wine Cellar
21. Colonel Wintle
22. Big Ben
23. Westminster Hall
24. The Bucklands
25. Birdcage Walk
26. The Blewcoat School

Shops made of ships' timbers, stuffed humans and, of course, zebras in the Mall!

Jeremy Bentham
Man in a Case

The philosopher Jeremy Bentham (1748–1832) was one of the great political and social thinkers of the later 18th and early 19th centuries. His many published works cover every subject from political reform to animal welfare, discussions of the state of the colonies and the evils of swearing. Most famously, he is associated with the idea of utilitarianism – the doctrine of the greatest good of the greatest number. Bentham was considered wildly eccentric in his day for advocating universal suffrage and the decriminalization of homosexuality. And he was closely involved in the idea of a 'dissenter's' university, which is what the University of London originally was. Dissenters – those who did not accept the supremacy of the Church of England – were not allowed to study at the old universities, so they set up their own.

The University started life in 1828 when Bentham was in his eighties, and though he took no practical part in establishing it he is often considered its spiritual father – largely because of his advocacy of religious tolerance and education for all. Bentham loved the new university, and bequeathed it all his manuscripts. He also left a legacy of unsurpassed

LEFT: *Centuries ahead of his time, Jeremy Bentham was both brilliant and eccentric, which may explain why he insisted on being stuffed after his death.*

PREVIOUS PAGE: *The gorgeous interior of the Café Royal, where writers and artists have dined in spendour for over a century.*

eccentricity. Visitors to the South Cloisters of the main building of University College (the main university as was) cannot fail to notice the large wood and glass cabinet that stands in the corridor.

Inside this is a surprisingly lifelike and life-size Jeremy Bentham, comfortably seated with a stick in his hand and dressed in the very clothes he wore in life. The figure is not a model: it is the actual preserved remains of the great man. When his remains were first put here following his death in 1832, the embalming technique used wasn't quite up to scratch, and the head deteriorated so badly that a wax replica had to be made. But beneath the clothing lurks his real skeleton, ensuring his continued presence in the academic world he so loved in life.

Legends about the preserved philosopher abound. One states that he used to be wheeled into every university council meeting. Another has it that for a decade before he died, Bentham carried around the glass eyes he wanted used in his preserved head. When they were eventually used for this purpose they fell out; then the head itself fell off and was found between Bentham's feet! Whatever the truth or otherwise of these and other stories (including the one about the students found playing football with the head!), we do know that in fact the real head is kept in the college vaults.

No one quite knows why Bentham stipulated in his will that he should be preserved and set up for public display in this way, but his decision fits neatly with the philosophy of a man who took a practical view of affairs and who thought it was important to make a contribution to the day-to-day life of the society in which he lived; he probably thought it would be nice, when his life ended, to be in some position where he could watch the world go by, and a cabinet in the cloisters is probably as good a place as any!

Berners Street
Celebrity Row

For more than a century after it was built – in the mid-1700s – this undistinguished-looking street attracted the rich and famous to an extraordinary degree. Virtually every house seems to have been lived in by a celebrity at one time or another.

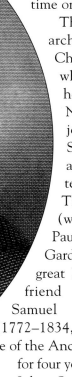

ABOVE: *Samuel Taylor Coleridge was both a poet and an opium addict, and he was just one of an extraordinary number of celebrities to live in Berners Street.*

The great British architect Sir William Chambers (1723–96), who built several houses here, lived at No. 53; he was joined by Sir Robert Smirke (1780–1867 and another architect) at No. 28 and Thomas Hardwick (who restored St Paul's Church, Covent Garden) at No. 55. The great Romantic poet and friend of Wordsworth, Samuel Taylor Coleridge (1772–1834, author of 'The Rime of the Ancient Mariner') lived for four years at No. 71, while John Opie (1761–1807), a talented painter from Cornwall, arrived in 1781 and lived at No. 8 for the next 15 years. Opie was best known for his portraits and for his pictures of children and country folk, and his talent earned him the sobriquet of 'the Cornish Wonder'. Sir Joshua Reynolds, first president of the Royal Academy, introduced Opie to wealthy patrons, and the two are buried side by side at St Paul's Cathedral.

Stanley Green
'Don't Eat Peanuts!'

ABOVE: *Loved by some, loathed by others, Stanley Green spent decades campaigning against the consumption of peanuts, peas, beans...*

OPPOSITE: *The distinctive mock-Tudor Liberty Hall, which is now one of the world's most famous shops, was actually built from recycled oak ships' timbers.*

Many of the artistic residents of Berners Street were considered highly eccentric, and they generated no end of anecdotes. One such is told by the history painter Benjamin Robert Haydon of a visit to the German painter Henry Fuseli (who lived at No. 13). Haydon knocked on the elderly Fuseli's door; after a considerable time the door slowly creaked open and 'A little bony hand slid round the door, followed by a little white-headed lion-faced man in an old flannel dressing gown tied round his waist with rope and on his head his wife's wickerwork sewing basket.'

The street's more notorious association is with Fauntleroy's Bank, which had its premises here in the 18th century until the founder, Henry Fauntleroy (1785–1824) was convicted of forgery and hanged at Tyburn.

Stanley Green died at the age of 78 in 1992, having spent nearly 30 years parading Oxford Street in London with a placard warning against the dangers of eating protein. He sold thousands of hand-printed leaflets (at 12p each) explaining why lustful feelings were induced by 'fish, birds, meat, cheese, egg, peas, beans, nuts and sitting'. 'Protein makes passion,' he would say to anyone who would listen. 'If we eat less of it, the world will be a happier place.'

Green had worked for many years in the Civil Service before starting his one-man campaign against lust in the mid-1960s. He produced his leaflets on a small press in his tiny flat in north-west London; the tenants below often complained about the terrific sounds of thumping and crashing on print day. Until he qualified for a pensioner's bus pass, he would cycle each day to Oxford Street in his raincoat, cap and wire-rimmed spectacles, and always recalled with pleasure that motorists reading the board on the back of his bicycle would toot their horns and wave. 'I've known coaches pass,' he said, 'and everyone has stood up and cheered me.'

He was occasionally spat at, but he was rarely upset by abuse, explaining that people only attacked him because they thought he was a religious person. He would often concentrate his efforts on cinema queues, using such attention-grabbing opening gambits as 'You cannot deceive your groom that you are a virgin on your wedding night'!

Liberty Hall
How Not to Get Lost

One of London's most famous shops since it was opened by Arthur Liberty, a Buckinghamshire draper, in 1875, Liberty – as it is now known – represented the ultimate in fashion between 1880 and 1920, and has long been associated with the Arts and Crafts Movement. The shop originally sold Japanese fans, silk and other fabrics – Mr Liberty was one of the first shopkeepers to import oriental goods in bulk. Success came quickly, owing in no small part to the decision of Messrs Gilbert and Sullivan to use Liberty fabrics

ABOVE: *A model ship acting as a weathervane perched atop the roof of Liberty Hall is a reminder of the shop's curious construction.*

ABOVE: *If it's true that the devil is in the detail, then the Café Royal must be a most wicked place, as its interior is almost overwhelmingly ornate.*

for the costumes in their light opera *Patience* (1881).

In 1925, flushed with success, the company – which had by now acquired three adjacent shops – decided to rebuild. The result was the extraordinary mock-Tudor building we see today facing Great Marlborough Street. On the side of the store that faces Regent Street, however, Liberty had to stick to the Portland stone from which the rest of the street is built.

Constructed round an interior courtyard, Liberty conceals a remarkable secret: it is built almost entirely from the magnificent oak timbers of two dismantled ships, HMS *Hindustan* and HMS *Impregnable*. The best craftsmen were hired – including several brought over specially from Italy – to install stained glass, magnificent staircases and superb carvings. Everything in the building is hand-made.

Perhaps the most delightfully eccentric thing about Liberty is that the siting of its staircases means the customers can easily become disoriented. In recognition of this fact, in the 1970s the owners published a booklet entitled *How Not To Get Lost in Liberty*!

Café Royal
Dining in Style

Visitors to London are often fooled by Regent Street. The great sweep of this magnificent thoroughfare was the brainchild of John Nash, who built Carlton House and the exquisite terraces bordering Regent's Park, but none of what we see today in Regent Street has anything to do with Nash.

Developers in the 1920s demolished almost every Nash building (with the exception of All Souls' Church) as well as the ornate colonnade that kept rain off the shoppers. The big, ugly buildings we now see are the work of a justly forgotten architect. Aside from All Souls', one feature of Nash's Regent Street survived by the skin of its teeth: the Grill Room at the Café Royal.

The Café Royal was opened in one of Nash's buildings by Daniel Thevenon, a Paris wine merchant, in 1870. It became so famous that artists, writers and film stars rarely visited London without

dropping in. When the remodelled street was proposed, the architects had every intention of building a new Café Royal, and were astonished when there was an outcry from across the world that the beautiful original was to be destroyed. After a long campaign, which included representations from the Royal Family, a compromise was reached: the interior of the dining room, with its magnificent decoration, would be carefully removed and slotted into place in the new building – and that is exactly what happened.

Today, if you are wealthy enough to afford lunch or dinner at the Café Royal, you can dine in an interior of deep red plush and golden cherubs that is the very same as that known and loved by everyone from Oscar Wilde to Augustus John, Lillie Langtry, J. M. Barrie and George Bernard Shaw.

ABOVE: *When Nash's Regent Street was rebuilt in the 1920s, the interior of the dining room at the Café Royal was carefully reinstated.*

Burlington Arcade
No Whistling or Running

One of the delights of London is that you can find odd, quirky little places hidden on the busiest of thoroughfares. Piccadilly must be one of the most famous streets in the world, and it is certainly busy, but just off it – and easy to miss – is a row of tiny Georgian shops virtually unchanged since they were completed in 1819.

Burlington Arcade exists for a most bizarre reason. Visitors might assume that the Georgian planners

ABOVE: *The tiny 18th-century shops of Burlington Arcade were built for the strange purpose of preventing commoners from throwing rubbish at Lord Cavendish.*

who built these little shops were simply building to make a profit. In fact, they built the arcade to cover a narrow alley that ran alongside Burlington House, now the home of the Royal Academy of Arts but which was then a private home. The owner of Burlington House was Lord Cavendish, who had complained for years that while sitting in his garden he was constantly hit on the head by oyster shells, apple cores, old bottles and even an occasional dead cat being tossed over the wall from the alleyway.

Cavendish decided that a row of shops would put paid to the nuisance. Samuel Ware was asked to design the beautiful shop fronts, and though the interiors are tiny the shopkeepers have always sold luxury goods, so what they lack in quantity of stock they more than make up for in quality. Originally, the arcade occupied a single storey, but an upper level was added in 1906 and the rooms above the shops were let to, according to one wag, 'the better sort of courtesan'. The beautiful

triple-arch entrance was destroyed in 1931, and the new design was much hated. There was also some damage during the Second World War, but the arcade – one of the world's first shopping malls – remains virtually intact. Instead of security guards it still has a 'beadle', who will ask you to leave if he catches you running or whistling or carrying an open umbrella!

Ritz Hotel
A Duck on the Roof

Until well into the 20th century it was quite common to see people on trains and buses carrying shotguns. In town a man carrying a shotgun case would arouse no comment at all, and in rural areas all sorts of people carried guns. They were not seen as a threat, but rather as an item of sporting equipment, much like a tennis racquet, or else as a tool of the countryman.

In the big London hotels, particularly in August, a man with several shotguns under his arm would probably be assumed to be an American on the first leg of a grouse-shooting visit. One American visitor

ABOVE: *If the beadle at Burlington Arcade catches you doing anything as outrageous as running or opening an umbrella, he will courteously ask you to leave.*

ABOVE: *Over the years, the Ritz Hotel has played host to many eccentric guests, but few as wacky as the American who went duck-shooting on the hotel roof.*

to the Ritz at the end of the 19th century had all the shooting equipment associated with the very rich: a pair of London guns, the very best shooting attire and two very expensive and well-trained dogs. But their owner was from a very rural part of the United States, where a man could pretty much walk out of the back door of his house and shoot whatever he liked. So, when the American visitor noticed small parties of geese and duck flying over the hotel each morning and evening, he thought that trying to shoot them was the most natural thing in the world.

Whether he bribed a porter or just managed to find his way to the hotel's rooftop by sheer good luck, is a mystery. On his first evening he fired two shots and missed both times, but he thought he had the measure of the thing and was convinced he'd have more luck the following evening. As it turned out, he was right. With his first shot he downed a mallard that landed behind the hotel. It is easy to imagine the

excited American running down the stairs and out into the street, asking the first passer-by if he or she had happened to see a duck fall out of the sky.

The American carried on shooting each evening for five days before an elderly hotel guest complained about the terrible noise emanating from the roof. The management had no idea what the guest was talking about, but they sent someone up the following evening who discovered what was going on. The hotel's reaction to these unusual goings-on is not recorded, but the shooting stopped and the American was soon on his way to Yorkshire.

The hotel management was probably more concerned about the possible disturbance to its other guests than to the actual act of shooting. After all, this was an era in which a Member of Parliament – whose identity has never been revealed – would spend several hours each week taking potshots at pigeons from his Whitehall office.

Fortnum and Mason
Keeping Time

One of London's last truly old-fashioned stores, Fortnum's still insists that the staff in its wine department wear frock coats. The shop's origins lie in the friendship between William Fortnum, a footman in the royal household, and shopkeeper Hugh Mason. As a footman to Queen Anne, one of Fortnum's jobs was to ensure that the candles in the palace candelabra were replaced regularly. He was allowed to keep the stumps of the old candles, and made a good living selling these on to the poor. Over the years he

BELOW: *The Fortnum and Mason clock has the unique peculiarity of having models of its founders bowing to each other each time the timepiece strikes the hour.*

also learned about what the royal household needed to buy on a regular basis, so when he retired he suggested to his friend Mason that they set up shop together supplying the palace and the gentry. The shop opened in 1707 in Piccadilly, near its present premises, and did so well that Mason established a team of horses and carts for deliveries.

By the end of the 18th century, Fortnum and Mason were famous for importing a vast range of wonderfully exotic foods from the East, largely through the rapidly expanding East India Company. Explorers and generals took Fortnum's potted meats and other foods with them on expeditions and campaigns, and soon the shop's famous hampers were being sent all over the world. Queen Victoria famously sent a huge Fortnum's vat of beef tea to Florence Nightingale in the Crimea, and the explorer William Parry set off in search of the North West Passage in 1819 with a casket of more

than two hundred-weight of Fortnum and Mason cocoa powder!

Sadly Fortnum and Mason's beautiful old shop was rebuilt in the 1920s, but an elaborate clock made in the 1960s and fitted to the Piccadilly front of the present store commemorates its Georgian origins. The clock shows the figures of Messrs Fortnum and Mason, and when it strikes the hour the two figures step out and bow to each other. The figure in the red coat is Fortnum – red being the dress colour for footmen of the royal household.

Traditions within the shop also hark back two centuries and more: the man in charge of the bakery, for example, is known as the Groom of the Pastry.

ABOVE: *The outrageous poet Lord Byron is just one of a number of celebrities who has lived in one of London's oldest and oddest blocks of flats.*

in London: acquiring a 'set' there (a flat at Albany is always known as a set) is not only down to money but also to influence and connections. Famous residents past and present are too numerous to list, but include British states-man Lord Palmerston (1784–1865), the out-landish poet Lord Byron (1788–1824), former Prime Minister William Gladstone (1809–98), novelist Aldous Huxley (1894–1963), the actress Dame Edith Evans (1888–1976), novelist Graham Greene (1904–91) and, in more recent times, the actor Stephen Fry (b. 1957).

Albany
In the Top Set

Designed by William Chambers in the 1770s, Melbourne House is one of the last of the great 18th-century mansions that once lined Piccadilly. Its name was changed to Albany (never *the* Albany) when its original owner, Lord Melbourne, swapped it for a house owned by Frederick Duke of York and Albany. The house was then remodelled by Henry Holland in 1802 in order to create 'select accommodation for bachelors', later to include single women.

Holland increased the size of the house by building two elegant blocks in the garden with a covered walk-way between them, known as the Rope Walk. Albany is still used to this day to house a 'select' clientele. It is without question one of the most exclusive addresses

Floris
The Sweet Smell of Success

The vast glasshouses (or 'Crystal Palace') built for the Great Exhibition held in Hyde Park in 1851 and subsequently moved to South London burned down in the 1930s, and there is almost nothing left, apart from engravings from the time, to remind us of that epoch-making event – one that celebrated the British Empire and the vast industrial workhouse that resulted from Britain's domination of world trade and enterprise. One tiny part of the Great Exhibition does still exist, though, in a little shop – itself of enormous historical interest – in Jermyn Street.

J. Floris is a Georgian perfumer that appears almost entirely unaffected by the modern world. The business was started in 1720 by a Spanish barber and 'smooth-pointed comb maker' from Menorca called Juan Floris. Having plied his trade for some years, Floris realized

that in an area of wealthy aristocrats, such as nearby St James's Square, a range of individually tailored perfumes would fare well. He began to experiment, and it is said that the perfumes he began to create were designed to remind him of the summer flowers of his homeland. They became enormously popular and the business flourished, and continues to do so today. By 1821, the firm had received a Royal Warrant, yet despite its enormous success – by the end of the 19th century it was exporting all over the world – it remained installed in the old-fashioned shop where it all began.

And what is the link with the Great Exhibition? Well, when you've marvelled at the beautiful brass and mahogany fittings in the shop, look closely at the display cases. Also carefully crafted in mahogany, these are the very same display cases as were used at the Great Exhibition. When the exhibition ended, the wily Floris family bought and transported them to Jermyn Street, where they have remained ever since.

Eros
Bows and Errors

Everything about this small yet world-famous statue in the centre of Piccadilly is odd. For a start, it is made from aluminium, a metal poorly suited to the wet British weather. And its Cupid-style bow is all wrong: bows of this type were strung on the opposite side to this one. As if that were not enough, the statue is also facing the wrong way – and in fact doesn't represent Eros at all!

The statue was the crowning glory of a fountain built at public expense in memory of one of London's great philanthropists, the seventh Earl of Shaftesbury (1801–85), after whom Shaftesbury Avenue is named. Shaftesbury spent much of his life and fortune clothing, feeding and educating the poor. The money for the fountain and statue was quickly raised, and Alfred Gilbert was commissioned to design the latter. Gilbert chose to depict the angel of Christian charity, but the angel's tell-tale bow led Londoners immediately to christen the figure Eros, after the Greek god of love. The statue was intended to aim its arrow up Shaftesbury Avenue, and although it has been turned to face in a number of different directions over the years, it has somehow never faced the right way. The statue was erected and the fountains turned

ABOVE: *Despite its fame, this sculpture of Eros is all wrong: not only is the bow being held the wrong way round, making it useless, but the figure isn't even Eros!*

OPPOSITE: *Step back in time to 19th-century London in Floris, the traditional perfumers. The cabinets are fine examples of British craftsmanship, made for the 1851 Great Exhibition.*

on in 1893, but the basin into which the water fell was too small and the force of water too great: passers-by were soaked, and the fountain had to be redesigned.

Alfred Gilbert, though now largely forgotten, was hugely influential in the 1880s, and was as eccentric and bohemian as the statue he designed. He argued about every stage of the work, hated the final result (particularly the fountain on which his sculpture stood) and told his patrons that they should take it down, melt it 'and make it into pence to give the unfortunate people who nightly find a resting place on the Thames embankment to the everlasting shame and disgrace of the metropolis of the world.' Often short of a penny himself, Gilbert accepted eleven commissions offered to him but hardly ever completed them: he would simply take on too much. He eventually fled the country to escape imprisonment for debt.

For the first half-century of its life, Eros became an unofficial market place: flower girls would gather here to sell their wares. They were a much-loved institution, but after the Second World War they never returned, and the statue is now no more than a meeting place, and a site where every tourist stops to have his or her photograph taken.

Lock & Co. Hatters and Berry Bros & Rudd
Heads Apart

St James's Street, that elegant sloping thoroughfare that leads from Piccadilly down to the Tudor Gateway of St James's Palace, was once a street of humble shops, before the rich built their grand houses and clubs. Two of these shops, by some small miracle, remain.

Berry Bros & Rudd began trading here at the end of the 17th century, and very little has changed in the intervening 300 years. Ancient floors and benches slope in every direction, and the walls are crooked, too. What is more, the business is still family-owned and run. Byron bought his wine here, as did Admiral Lord Nelson (1758–1805) and the Duke of Wellington (1769–1852), followed by the actor Laurence Olivier (1907–89) and novelist Evelyn Waugh (1903–66).

Running down one side of the shop is an ancient lane that leads to a tiny secluded courtyard – London was once a dense network of tiny lanes and courtyards. This is one of the last remaining, and the beautiful houses that surround it all date from the 1720s. Curiously, they were built by one William Pickering, a relative of the Berry brothers.

Lock & Co., just a few doors down from Berry Bros, has been making hats in London since the 17th century, and has occupied this shop since 1764. Its interiors and fixtures have changed little. Creaking timber shelves display hats of all kinds, and the shop still uses an extraordinary device – a conformator – to measure each client's head: the details, including distinguishing lumps and bumps, are kept on file so that new hats can be made to order even if the customer is on the other side of the world.

Lock's have made hats for just about everyone, from Nelson to Charlie Chaplin, and have even earned literary immortality, being mentioned in John Betjeman's great autobiographical poem 'Summoned by Bells'. Most famously, they invented the bowler hat, which was, until the 1960s, *de rigueur* for male office workers in the City of London. The bowler actually started life as a gamekeeper's hat: it was designed for the immensely wealthy Lord Coke of Norfolk, whose gamekeepers were occasionally attacked by poachers and needed some sort of protective headgear. How the hat made the transition to the Square Mile is something of a mystery.

79 Pall Mall
Mistress in the House

Pall Mall, which runs from St James's Palace to Trafalgar Square, is one of the most historic in London. It gets its name from the Italian *pallamaglio* – meaning 'ball and mallet' – a game that came to England in the

ABOVE: *Hats of all shapes, sizes and styles can be found at Lock & Co., where the bowler hat was invented specifically for Lord Coke's gamekeepers.*

OPPOSITE: *The old shopfronts of Berry Bros & Rudd and Lock & Co. in St James's Street conceal equally ancient interiors and original fittings.*

ABOVE: *Charles I's best-loved mistress Nell Gwynn was gifted the only freehold property in Pall Mall.*

17th century and was played in St James's Park by Charles II (1630–85) and his mistresses; it was an unstructured and rather energetic version of croquet.

Today, the street is made up almost entirely of offices and clubs, but it was once one of London's most fashionable addresses, and as a result of the bizarre workings of royal patronage and favour it contains a unique building: No. 79. This is the only building in the whole street whose freehold is not owned by the Crown. And the reason? The house that originally stood on the site was owned by none other than Charles II's favourite mistress, Nell Gwynn (1650–87).

When Charles offered to find Nell a house near St James's Palace, No. 79 happened to be free. Charles gave her a long lease and thought no more about it. She refused to move in, though, on the grounds, as she apparently put it, that she had 'always conveyed free under the Crown and always would.' In other words, unless she had the freehold, the deal – and probably much besides – was off. Charles knew when he was beaten and arranged to have the freehold given to Nell. When she died, her son, the Duke of St Alban's (Charles made him duke after hearing Nell shout at him 'Come here, you little bastard!'), inherited the freehold, and it was later sold to pay off his debts. It has been bought and sold ever since without returning to the Crown.

Walter Rothschild
The Original Zebra Crossing!

Decidedly but brilliantly eccentric, Lionel Walter Rothschild (1868–1937) hated speaking to people, was blackmailed out of a fortune by his mistress and trained four zebras to pull his carriage along Pall Mall. Unfitted for the normal routes into public life that Rothschild elder sons tended to take, he instead opened a natural-history museum which eventually grew to be the biggest private museum in the world.

Rothschild would pay almost anything for a rare or unusual specimen, and by 1920, after working in virtual seclusion for years for 18 hours a day, he had amassed some 2,000 complete mounted animals, along with 200 heads, 300 antlers, 3,000 stuffed birds, 700 reptiles, 1,000 fish, 300,000 bird skins and 200,000 birds' eggs. He was a brilliant, if utterly obsessive, classifier.

On one famous occasion, while being driven through Hyde Park, Rothschild spotted a chauffeur standing beside a stationary car with a folded rug over his arm. Rothschild immediately shouted at his own driver to stop. He leapt from the car, explaining that the rug in the other chauffeur's arms was made from the pelts of tree kangaroos; he then waited until the owner of the rug arrived, and refused to leave until the rug had been sold to him.

Financial troubles eventually led Walter to sell part of his great collection. So upset was he by this that he quickly fell ill and died within a few months.

ABOVE AND RIGHT: *George III's son Frederick, Duke of York had only one talent: running up debts, and jokes abounded that this monolith was built to keep him safe from creditors.*

Duke of York's Column
High Flyer

One of the most curious monuments in London, the Duke of York's column, just off The Mall, was built to commemorate Frederick, second son of George III, a man who did little more than run up huge debts. Despite the fact that Frederick was a member of the Royal Family, no financial backer for his monument could be found. Eventually the government decided, without consultation, to raise funds by docking one day's pay from every soldier in the British Army.

Thus some of the poorest subjects in the land were forced to pay the sum of £25,000 for a monument to one of the nation's richest and most profligate aristocrats. But Frederick, in the end, paid a price of sorts: from the moment it was completed in 1824, the monument became the butt of jokes: a favourite for many years was that Frederick's column had to be as high as it is (124 feet/38 metres) so that Londoners wouldn't have to put up with the stink of the duke on top of it; another popular jibe was that the column had to be exceptionally high to protect Frederick from his creditors.

ABOVE: *Refreshments are now available in St James's Park in the modern Inn in the Park, but only because of a peculiar quirk of history.*

Milkmaids in St James's
Parklife

London's parks are among its chief glories. The oldest – St James's – was originally established as a hunting ground so that kings and courtiers could hunt deer from the nearby palaces of St James's and Westminster. One of the strangest stories associated with St James's Park concerns the café that stands near the lake.

The story begins in 1905, when London's planners decided to build the grand semicircular Admiralty Arch. The arch was designed to take up only a small area of land, but there was a problem. Two elderly women had walked to this corner with their three cows every day for as long as anyone could remember. They would tether the cows and set up their stall: for a penny a glass, passers-by could enjoy a drink of fresh milk. It was a treat much enjoyed by Londoners and visitors alike, and the two women made a very good

living. But their place of business was in the way of the new arch, and the authorities were not going to let the old ladies impede progress. They were told to remove themselves forthwith, but word leaked to the press, and the public was up in arms: questions were raised in Parliament, and the great and the good penned articles in the newspapers expressing their outrage at the notion of abolishing one of the most delightful traditions associated with the park. What clinched it was that Edward VII (1901–1910) remembered drinking at the ladies' corner, and he too thought it was a scandal that they should be ousted.

The only snag was that the ladies had no paperwork to prove their claim that there was an ancient right to sell milk in the park. However, they insisted that their families had sold milk in this spot since the mid-17th century, and researchers eventually uncovered a long history of milk-selling in the park. It became increasingly difficult to justify the removal of these two milkmaids and their cows.

At last the planners relented and the ladies were allowed to stay – provided they moved down to the lake. They were also told that the right to sell milk in the park would die with them. In the end, this did not quite happen: the last of the two women died in about 1920, but the sale of refreshments lived on. A restaurant selling a whole range of food and drink stands today on the spot where the two milkmaids once plied their trade, exercising what seems by its very longevity to have become a right.

Craig's Court
Stuck in a Rut

Near the top of Whitehall, a hundred yards or so from Trafalgar Square where Nelson looks down from his column towards Westminster Abbey and the Houses of Parliament, lies a little-known alleyway with a bizarre history.

As you walk down Whitehall from Trafalgar Square, Craig's Court is found on the left. It runs into a small square or courtyard, where a replica of the façade of Harrington House, built in 1702 for the Earl

of Harrington, still stands; the earl built his house here just a few years after a huge fire destroyed the medieval palace of Whitehall.

Harrington was convinced that Whitehall Palace would be rebuilt after the fire: building his own house so close to it would leave his family perfectly poised to visit the court every day and seek patronage. Unluckily for Harrington, however, the palace was never rebuilt. His red-brick house was destined to stare forlornly at the houses of lesser men than the king, but, tucked away down a blind alley, it (or at least its façade) escaped successive waves of redevelopment. By the 1950s the interior had been remodelled several times and the house was being used as a telephone exchange, but even today the exterior is much as it would have been in the early 18th century.

When you've looked at the house, look down at the surface of the narrow alleyway, for here, in a sense, is where's London's pavements have their origins. Until the mid-18th century, London's streets had no pavements. Cart and carriage drivers could drive as near to the walls of houses as they liked. This made going for a walk a dangerous business; it also meant that in particularly narrow streets carriages

ABOVE: *The popular tourist destination of Horse Guards is actually the former entrance to a vanished palace.*

occasionally got stuck between the houses. Kerbstones and pavements began to appear after the then speaker of the House of Commons, Mr Onslow, got stuck in Craig's Court after a visit to Harrington's house. After attempts to dislodge the carriage failed, a red-faced and, by all accounts, extremely angry Mr Onslow had to be extricated through a hole cut in the carriage's roof. He returned to Parliament on foot, and when the next debate on the state of the capital's streets was held, Onslow helped vote through a bill that compelled each householder in London to pay for a row of kerbstones in front of his or her house.

Horse Guards
Military Manoeuvres

Every visitor to London makes a beeline for the Horse Guards, those brightly uniformed mounted soldiers who stoically ignore the ever-present throng of tourists eager to have their photographs taken alongside this small piece of living history.

ABOVE: *Henry VIII's jousting ground was situated close to the present-day Horse Guards Parade.*

The guards' presence at the entrance to Horse Guards Parade, halfway up Whitehall, dates back at least to the time of Charles II. This part of Whitehall was also where Henry VIII had his jousting ground and where his guards lived when the old Palace of Westminster stretched from present-day Parliament Square almost as far as Trafalgar Square. The two mounted guards outside the present Horse Guards building (completed in 1750) defend this route into the palace precincts – despite the fact that the palace is long gone.

Monarchs have reviewed their troops on the Parade since the early 16th century. Reach it by passing beneath the arch, and then turn left to the corner of the parade ground, where you will see a doorway (now sadly closed for security reasons). This conceals a covered passageway that runs from the parade ground to Downing Street, and has been here since at least the 18th century. The walls of the passage were traditionally painted white because the route was unlit and what little light filtered through would be magnified, it was hoped, by the bright walls. Records suggest that the last time the walls were painted was at the end of the 19th century, but for more than a decade afterwards the sentry who guarded the entrance to the passageway was told to shout 'Keep to the left!' to prevent the important personages who used the route getting white paint on their clothes.

Henry VIII's Wine Cellar
The King's Tipple

It is difficult now to visualize Whitehall and the Palace of Westminster as they were before the building of Parliament Square and the present Houses of Lords and Commons. All along the river here was a warren of royal buildings stretching back to Westminster Abbey and up Whitehall to Banqueting Hall. Westminster Palace was never one great building: it was a mass of small, ramshackle buildings dating back to the time of William the Conqueror.

Henry VIII (1491–1547) got so fed up with its shabby appearance that when Cardinal Wolsey fell from grace, the king appropriated the Cardinal's huge house further up Whitehall and changed its name from York Place to Whitehall Palace. Many of the old royal buildings along Whitehall had been demolished by the time a huge fire destroyed almost everything in 1834, but the Banqueting Hall (1619–22) survived, as did the Jewel Tower and what is now known as Henry VIII's wine cellar.

The cellar is the only surviving part of Wolsey's old palace, which was built, it is thought, at the end of the 15th century. What makes the cellar's survival extraordinary is the fact that when Whitehall was being rebuilt in the 1950s the cellar was spared demolition: instead, the vaulted undercroft, supported by four massive octagonal pillars and weighing more than 800 tons, was carefully lowered 18 feet (5.5 metres) to preserve it beneath the foundations of a modern office building.

Not a brick or stone was damaged during this remarkable – and expensive – procedure: the bill mounted to more than £100,000, which would equate to many millions of pounds in today's terms.

Colonel Wintle
The Military Eccentric

Lieutenant Colonel Alfred Daniel Wintle, who was to become one of London's greatest eccentrics, was born in 1897 in Russia, where his father was a diplomat. In spite of his Russian birth, or perhaps because of it, Wintle always claimed that he thanked God each night for making him an Englishman: being an Englishman was, he said, 'the highest responsibility as well as the greatest honour.'

As soon as the First World War (1914–18) started, Wintle joined up. On his first day in the trenches the soldier next to him was killed. Wintle was so terrified that he stood stock still and then saluted. 'That did the trick,' he said later, 'and within 30 seconds I had again become an English man of action.' A few months later he narrowly missed being killed himself when a shell blew him off his horse. He lost his left eye and most of his left hand, but he was apparently more concerned about the welfare of his horse – he adored horses and riding – and was relieved to hear that it was unharmed. The armistice failed to console him, however: he was convinced that the Germans were merely lying low, and he spent years lobbying Whitehall officials until they could stand it no more and he was posted from central London to Ireland.

By 1938, Wintle was back in the heart of Whitehall working in military intelligence. He was appalled at the official insistence that there would be no war. Once war did indeed begin, Wintle made strenuous efforts to see active service, even though by this time he was well into middle age. He presented himself at medical boards, disguising the fact that he had only one eye; but it did no good. He then attempted to get to France by impersonating a senior officer and trying to steal an aeroplane. This led to a court martial as Commodore Boyle – the man Wintle had tried to impersonate – decided to prosecute. Unabashed, Wintle visited Boyle at his Ministry of Defence office, waved a gun at him, and berated him for doing so little. Next morning, Wintle was arrested and taken to the Tower of London. Eventually, Wintle got his way: he found himself back in the saddle in North Africa, and then – as a fluent speaker of French and German – he was sent to work undercover in Nazi-occupied France.

ABOVE: *Colonel Wintle was one of London's most eccentric characters – and the bane of military chiefs in Whitehall.*

At the end of the war, Wintle retired and began his last great battle – this time on behalf of his sister, Marjorie. She had looked after a wealthy elderly relative of Wintle's, Kitty Wells, for more than 20 years. When Kitty died it was found that she had left her considerable fortune not to Marjorie but to her solicitor, Frederick Nye. The will was hugely complex and Wintle believed it had been drawn up by Nye deliberately to cheat Kitty. Wintle landed himself back in prison after kidnapping and humiliating Nye, but emerged undaunted. He took Nye to court, lost and was bankrupted, yet still persisted. He appealed to the House of Lords and spent three days presenting his own case: to the astonishment of everyone, he won!

Big Ben
Clocking In

Big Ben is one of London's oddest buildings. Like the rest of the Palace of Westminster it was built by Charles Barry (1795–1860) and Augustus Pugin

ABOVE: *Big Ben, which is officially known as St Stephen's Tower, with 'Ben' referring only to the bell. It was built after an acrimonious competition.*

about who should make the clock itself. The job was first offered to Benjamin Vulliamy, the Queen's clock-maker, who was based in Pall Mall. His design was attacked by fellow clockmaker E.J. Dent, however, so the commissioners charged with organizing the work launched a competition to design and build the new clock. The contract finally went to Dent, amid much acrimony, in 1852. Two years later, the clock – 15½ feet long by nearly 5 feet wide (5 by 1.5 metres) – was ready, but the tower was not. An East London company cast the great 16-ton bell, but during tests it cracked, and had to be melted down and recast, this time by another East London firm, the Whitechapel Bell Foundry. It took 16 horses the best part of a day to haul the gigantic bell to Parliament Square before it could be hoisted into position at the top of the tower.

When the clock began to run, it was discovered that the 2½-ton hands were so heavy that the mechanism could not move them. They were redesigned in a lighter metal but now crashed down past the three each time they reached 12. Remade for a third time in hollow copper, they worked – and they have kept time accurately ever since.

There are two theories surrounding the origins of the name 'Big Ben'. At around the time the clock was due to be completed, the prizefighter and publican Ben Caunt went 60 rounds with the best bare-knuckle boxer in the country, Nat Langham. The bout was declared a draw, but it made national heroes of both men. Ben Caunt was a huge man, and the great bell could have been named after him. The other story, however, attributes the name to Benjamin Hall, the government's chief commissioner of works, who was addressing the House on the subject of a name for the new bell tower when, to great laughter, someone shouted 'Call it Big Ben!'

Perhaps the most remarkable thing about the clock is that, even by the standards of today's supreme timepieces, it is remarkably accurate. When the commissioners launched their competition to design it, they stipulated that it must be accurate to within one second an hour; most clockmakers at the time agreed that this was impossible, but that is how accurate the clock still is today. In the rare event that it does get slightly out of time, a tiny coin, kept especially for the purpose, is placed on the huge pendulum, as the weight of the coin is enough to adjust the clock by a fraction of a second.

(1812–52) after a nationwide competition to find a new design for the seat of government following the disastrous fire of 1834. The late Georgian passion for Gothic gave Barry's design a head start, and work soon began on building the famous clock tower.

All the statistics to do with St Stephen's Tower (as Big Ben is properly named: the nickname actually refers to the bell inside the tower) and its great clock are astonishing. The tower is nearly 320 feet (97.5 metres) high, and more than two decades elapsed between the laying of the first foundation stone and starting the clock, largely because no one could agree

Westminster Hall
Roof Repairs

The lower parts of the walls of Westminster Hall are unchanged since this huge building was begun shortly after the Norman Conquest of 1066. What we see further up the building was finally completed in 1399.

The hall houses one of the greatest architectural treasures of the late Middle Ages: a vast, intricate and magnificent hammer-beam roof. Like any ancient building, Westminster Hall has required repair now and then: parts of the walls have been rebuilt or repaired, along with the windows, in earlier centuries; the roof too has been renewed here and there as the ancient timbers have decayed, and one section had to be replaced after an IRA bomb caused some damage in the 1980s.

The last major period of restoration was in 1913, when several major timbers were renewed. This presented the board of works with a major headache. England's oak woods had long since been felled, and officials simply could not find a plantation of oaks large enough to provide the right sort of timber; those that did exist were generally no more than two or three hundred years old, and were simply not big enough. Then someone had the bright idea of checking where the original timbers had come from. It was discovered that they had been brought to Westminster at the end of the 14th century from an estate near Wadhurst in Sussex. The estate had been owned at that time by the Courthorpe family.

As it happened, Sir George Courthorpe, a descendant of the Courthorpe family was, in 1913, Member of Parliament for Rye, the beautiful former Cinque Port on the south coast. When he was approached, Sir George astonished officials with the following

ABOVE: *One of the most extraordinary survivals in London is the roof construction of Westminster Hall, a monument to long-term planning!*

story. He explained that when the original trees had been cut down and sold to the king in the 14th century, his ancestors had imagined that a time would come when the timbers would need repair or renewal, and so they had planted a new stand of oaks specifically for the purpose. Those trees were now ready, and they were duly cut and used to repair the great roof of Westminster Hall.

ABOVE: *The Bucklands' house in London was always filled with exotic animals. However, when their pets died the family simply ate them.*

The Bucklands
A *Houseful of Animals*

William Buckland (1784–1856) was Dean of Westminster and a fanatical animal collector, whose house in London was crammed with thousands of natural-history specimens, both dead and alive; some of the latter shared his bed, and some he would eat after their death.

To prove the efficacy of bird droppings as fertilizer, Buckland once used great quantities of them to write the word 'guano' on the lawn at his Oxford college; when summer came the grass had indeed grown well and the letters could be seen clearly. At his house you were liable to be offered such exotic fare as roast hedgehog or grilled crocodile steak, and in all likelihood the meal comprised a former pet!

Frank Buckland (1826–80), William's son, was, if anything, even more eccentric than his father. He too was a naturalist and collector of animals, and he helped found the Society for the Acclimatisation of Animals in the United Kingdom, which introduced exotic fauna in an attempt, it was said, to expand the roast-beef diet of the British.

Buckland was appointed Her Majesty's Inspector of Fisheries, and in this capacity was responsible for making sure that migratory fish were able to get up Britain's rivers. While helping construct a salmon ladder on the Thames he put up a sign for the benefit of any salmon stuck in the weir below the as-yet unbuilt ladder: 'No road at present over the weir,' it read. 'Go downstream, take the first turning to the right and you will find good travelling water upstream and no jumping required.'

On another occasion, fascinated by the salmon's ability to swim against a fierce current, Buckland stripped off and plunged into the river to feel the strength of the current for himself.

Stories of Buckland's strange ways abound. Like his father, he filled his house with creatures of every shape and size. He was fascinated with them – whether living or dead: the stench from the house was notorious. But his obsession with animals was founded on a profound respect for them. He campaigned for many years for humane methods of slaughter in abattoirs and he disliked intensely the indiscriminate slaughter of animals for sport.

Birdcage Walk
Birdspotting

Casual visitors and tourists who notice the curious name of this street probably imagine that it commemorates the keeping of birds here – perhaps in cages hanging from the elegant windows of the tall houses overlooking St James's Park. They would be almost, though not quite, right. Birdcage Walk in fact marks the site of a royal aviary.

Built by James I (1566–1625), the aviary was doubled in size by his grandson Charles II (1630–85). Neither king was known for his love of budgerigars, however: the aviary housed the royal falcons and hawks, birds kept specifically for hunting. The Walk is now a wide, busy road, but it was once a route that had to be walked by all bar the king and the Hereditary Grand Falconer, who alone were allowed to drive their carriages here. This rule was rigidly adhered to until 1828: when the route was opened to lesser mortals, the downfall of the Empire, no less, was predicted.

The houses that line Birdcage Walk are some of the earliest still standing in central London, and constitute the best complete group of Queen Anne houses in the capital. They were built at the very beginning of the 18th century, and what you see from the Walk are actually the backs of the houses.

The Blewcoat School
Back to the Books

Just around the corner from Victoria Street with its glass and steel 1960s tower blocks is an odd little building that seems to sit at an awkward angle, neither parallel to the road nor at right angles to it. The building – small, symmetrical, red-brick and rather Dutch looking – is The Blewcoat School, which was erected here back in an era when the environs of Westminster Abbey, a few hundred yards away, constituted the biggest slum in London, and the route down to Victoria was via an unpaved track.

The school was established in 1688 for the education of 'fifty poor boys likely to thrive by scholarship'. The founder's stipulation was that the boys must all be from the parish of St Mary's (the church that stands today right next to Westminster Abbey), and they were to be taught to read, write and cast accounts. A local brewer, William Greene, paid for the building, which stood (as it still does) on land rented from the church. Remarkably for the time, girls were admitted – 'to the number of 20' – in 1713. They were subsequently ousted – no one seems to know why – in the 1870s, but the building continued in use as a school until 1939. Above the front door is a life-size painted woodcarving of a Blewcoat schoolboy, in his blue coat. The strangely beautiful little building is now owned by the National Trust.

BELOW: *Looking oddly adrift amid later developments, the Blewcoat School is a reminder of Westminster's village past.*

Covent Garden

Covent Garden was once a solemn, quiet place that heard only the sounds of
nuns at prayer and curlews crying from the meadows that led to the river, but with
the dissolution of the monasteries and the never-ceasing spread of London it was caught
up in the rush and turmoil of the capital and, having been a vegetable market for
centuries, is now one of the liveliest and most popular tourist venues in London.
But beneath the veneer of modern shops and restaurants is a rich history of the odd,
the quirky and the downright eccentric.

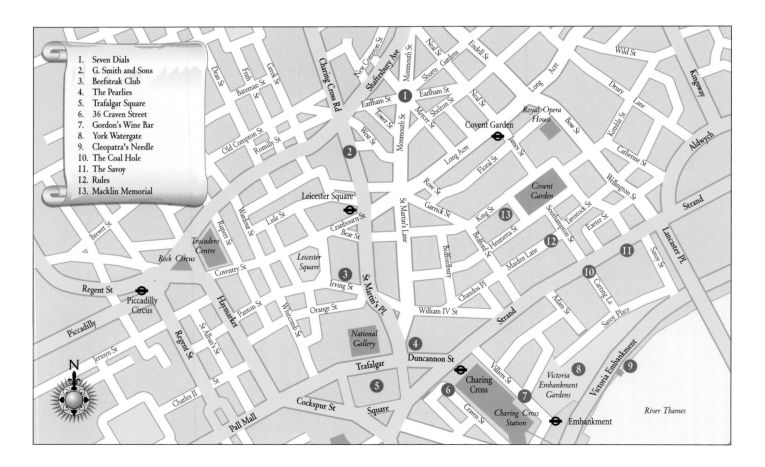

1. Seven Dials
2. G. Smith and Sons
3. Beefsteak Club
4. The Pearlies
5. Trafalgar Square
6. 36 Craven Street
7. Gordon's Wine Bar
8. York Watergate
9. Cleopatra's Needle
10. The Coal Hole
11. The Savoy
12. Rules
13. Macklin Memorial

Back-to-front streets, drunken beefsteaks and treasure troves

Seven Dials
Down at Tom-All-Alone's

Seven Dials, in the parish of St Giles-in-the-Fields, is one of the oddest and most interesting parts of London. Tucked away between Covent Garden to the south and Bloomsbury to the north, it miraculously escaped wholesale redevelopment in the 1960s and now bears only a few scars from that unenlightened period.

A medieval leper hospital existed here amid open fields until the first developers came in the 17th century. They put up houses for artisans and skilled tradesmen, but within a few decades an area that had seemed a model development to the diarist Samuel Pepys when he visited it, had degenerated into a dark, overcrowded and fearsome place.

The name Seven Dials comes from the place, in the southern part of the district, where seven small streets meet to form a star. The obelisk at the centre of the star where the seven streets meet is a modern replacement, but from here narrow streets of the 18th century and one or two earlier houses radiate towards Covent Garden, Charing Cross Road, Shaftesbury Avenue and Long Acre. There is still a small market here every weekday, which has been here for more than a century. Charles Dickens (1812–70) called the area Tom-All-Alone's in his novel *Bleak House*, and something of the atmosphere Dickens must have known still lingers.

The old road to Oxford (now Oxford Street) runs along what is now the northern extremity of the district, and it passes close by the parish church of St Giles, patron saint of lepers. For centuries church officials paid for a last drink at the Resurrection Gate inn for the condemned who passed the church and pub as they took their journey by cart from Newgate Prison in the east to the gallows at Tyburn (now Marble Arch) in the west. The inn (rebuilt in the 19th century and renamed the Angel Inn) still stands next to St Giles's Church. This was completed in 1712 after the earlier church began to collapse. St Giles is one of a tiny number of London churches that escaped Victorian 'improvements' and bombing in the Second World War (1939–45).

The plague of 1665, probably the worst outbreak in the whole history of that terrible disease, began in this area. By the 18th century, when Willliam Hogarth (1697–1764) depicted the area in his famous engraving *Gin Lane*, this was a place avoided by anyone the least bit respectable. It was also considered beyond the reach of the authorities.

Gin shops abounded, and poverty and desperation made the inhabitants widely feared. If a criminal from the area was being taken from Newgate to Tyburn, extra soldiers were often drafted in to guard him because, as likely as not, his friends would mount a rescue operation as he stopped for his last drink at the Resurrection Gate; and once he'd been carried off into the Rookeries, as Seven Dials was then known – the name deriving from all the tiny rooms filled with families, like rooks' nests – he would never be found.

Much of the original Rookeries area was destroyed in the 1880s to make way for Shaftesbury Avenue and New Oxford Street, but there is still much of interest. From the obelisk, walk up Monmouth Street, and after about 100 yards (110 metres) turn right into Neal's Yard – an enchanting courtyard containing shops and cafés. Also from the obelisk, cut down

ABOVE: *William Hogarth's engraving* Gin Lane *captured the grim essence of one of 18th-century London's most notorious districts: Seven Dials.*

OPPOSITE: *At the heart of Seven Dials – called Tom-All-Alone's by Charles Dickens – is the obelisk from which the area gets its name.*

PREVIOUS PAGES: *Cleopatra's Needle on the Embankment has nothing at all to do with the great Egyptian queen.*

through Earlham Street and cross Long Acre. Go through Banbury Court into the old carriage hall, then bear right a short distance until you turn left into Lazenby Court. This medieval alleyway takes you under – yes *under* – the 16th-century Lamb and Flag pub and is little more than 2 feet (0.5 metres) wide.

G. Smith & Sons
Snuff Shop Extraordinaire

G. Smith and Sons have been selling tobacco and snuff from their tiny shop in Shaftesbury Avenue since 1874. The shop is beautifully fitted out in the high Victorian style, and sells a vast range of pipes and tobaccos as well as the kind of snuff that would have been much in demand until about 1900. Very few people now take snuff but Smith still has a ready clientele. In fact, his is one of the last shops in the world to supply the ground-up powdered tobacco that was once taken virtually countrywide.

Snuff shopfronts traditionally displayed a wooden model of a man in Highland dress. Why this is, no one seems to know, but the tradition is an ancient one. The last full-size snuff Highlander stood outside the long-vanished snuff shop of Miller and Co. in Bedford Street. The shop closed in 1982, and the Highlander was packed off to a museum. All London

snuff shops – and there were dozens in the City alone in Victorian times – would have had a Highlander, but this created huge problems for the trade after the Jacobite rising of 1745. All things Scottish were banned, or at least frowned upon, but the snuff trade could not bear to give up its ancient tradition – which may explain the appearance in several London newspapers of the following extraordinary notice:

'We hear that the dapper wooden Highlanders who guard so heroically the doors of snuff-shops intend to petition the Legislature in order that they may be excused from complying with the act of Parliament with regard to their change of dress; alleging that they have ever been faithful subjects to His Majesty, having constantly supplied his Guards with a pinch out of their Mulls when they marched by them, and so far from engaging in any Rebellion, that they have never entertained a rebellious thought; whence they humbly hope that they shall not be put to the Expense of buying new cloaths.'

ABOVE, LEFT AND OPPOSITE: *It may be hard to believe now, but snuff (ground tobacco) was once taken by both children and adults and by dukes and the destitute. In the heart of London's Theatreland, G. Smith & Sons, continues to sell a range of snuffs, but gone is the wooden model of a Scotsman (right) that was the traditional sign of the snuff seller.*

Beefsteak Club
Clubbing Together

The Beefsteak Club started life as the Beef Steak Society. The society was founded in 1735 by John Rich, who ran the Covent Garden Theatre, and George Lambert, a scene painter, and originally membership was limited to 24. The members called themselves 'the steaks', and met every Saturday at 5pm from November to June.

Steak was the only thing on the menu, the idea being to celebrate beef and the liberty of the English. The club, which still exists, originally met in a room above the Lyceum Theatre, but by the 1980s had moved to No. 9 Irving Street, WC2. Early members were described as 'noblemen and gentlemen', and these days politicians, actors and writers have become members. One of the club's more delightful eccentricities is that members have always insisted on addressing all waiters – and waitresses – as Charles!

The Pearlies
King of the Costers

London's Pearly kings and queens are one of the capital's oddest yet most delightful sights. The origins of the pearly king and queen tradition are uncertain but we do know that it all began in Victorian times when a few of London's costermongers – street sellers of fruit and vegetables – began sewing mother-of-pearl buttons on to the edges of their bellbottom trousers.

Quite why they did this is a mystery – one theory says that a coster family took delivery of a particularly large box of mother of pearl buttons from the Far East (via the East End docks), and rather than waste the buttons it began to use them for decoration.

The fashion caught on and became connected with the costers' tradition of electing 'kings' to lead them against other market traders whenever there was trouble. The costers had a reputation for fierceness unmatched even in the tough world of the

ABOVE: *Could this be the world's smallest police station? The lock-up in Trafalgar Square.*

The highlight of the Pearly year is the Harvest Festival Service at the church of St Martins-in-the-Fields in the autumn when the pearlies gather in their finest and the Pearly princesses carry bouquets – not of flowers but of gorgeous vegetables – into the church. A sight not to be missed!

Trafalgar Square
Lions and Lock-ups

The creation of Trafalgar Square in the 1830s spelt the end of the ancient royal mews, where the king's falcons, and later his horses and coaches, were kept. By all accounts the area, which includes the land on which the National Gallery now stands, was ramshackle and semi-derelict by 1820, and few tears were shed for the wholesale demolition recommended by architect John Nash (1752–1835). Nash had suggested laying out Trafalgar Square as part of his grand plan to build a great, almost triumphal, road from Carlton House on The Mall up through Piccadilly.

Curiously, this grand plan included a decidedly eccentric little detail. At the south-east corner of Trafalgar Square, and missed by almost every tourist who comes here, is Britain's (possibly the world's) smallest police station. The structure looks like a rather fat lamp post and it is only on closer inspection that one notices the tiny door and window; there is barely room for two people to stand upright inside. It is said that this tiny lock-up had – and still has – a direct telephone link to Scotland Yard.

The other eccentric thing about Trafalgar Square is the story of its famous lions. When Nelson's column was being built, an artist had to be found to design the four huge lions round the base of the column. Queen Victoria wanted Edwin Landseer, one of her favourite painters, to carry out the work, but Landseer was horrified at the suggestion. He was not a sculptor and could bring no useful experience to bear on the commission. He refused, but the queen persisted. Landseer finally agreed, but only on the condition that he could take as long as he needed, and also that a dead lion or two be sent round to his studio so that he could study it before setting to work. Several months passed before a lion obligingly died (one hopes of natural causes) at London Zoo, and its corpse was immediately sent round to Landseer's

19th-century street trader and soon their kings (and their wives) were the ones wearing so many mother-of-pearl buttons that they seemed to be covered from head to foot.

Long after street trading changed beyond all recognition, the traditions of the pearlies continued and do so to this day, with Pearly kings and queens still 'reigning' in various parts of London. On Derby Day at Epsom Racecourse on the southern approaches to London, the Pearly King and Queen arrive in a magnificent decorated donkey cart – a delightful parody of the arrival of Royalty at similar events.

The Pearlies' suits – which gleam and shimmer with as many as 30,000 buttons (and weigh a ton!) – are handed down from parents to their children and Pearlies all over London are regularly invited to weddings and christenings. They also do an enormous amount for various charities.

house, where he kept it until it stank so badly that the neighbours began to complain. More than a year later, his plans for the splendid lions were ready.

The lions were finally installed some 25 years late. When Landseer died, wreaths were draped around their necks as a mark of respect.

36 Craven Street
The Benefits of Air Bathing

Benjamin Franklin (1706–90), one of the four signatoies of the American Declaration of Independence, lived for 16 years in a crooked little terraced house in Craven Street – a street that, before the building of the Embankment in the 1860s, ran down to the river. Craven Street survived not only the building of the Embankment (which effectively pushed the river back 200 yards/180 metres) but also the building of Charing Cross Station and the German bombs of the Second World War. Virtually all the houses in the street are 18th century, although most have been refurbished to create office space. No. 36, Franklin's old home, is one of the few to have survived with its interior virtually intact: what we see today are the very doors, chimney pieces and staircases once used by the man himself.

Franklin was a great friend of Erasmus Darwin, Mathew Boulton and Josiah Wedgwood, all of whom were members of the Lunar Society, a Midlands-based dining club of industrialists who embraced every new invention of the late 18th century, the first great period of the Industrial Revolution. Franklin was passionate about science long before he became passionate about American politics. He was also a noted eccentric, and had you wandered along Craven Street early in the 18th century on a summer's day you might well have seen him sitting at his drawing-room window completely naked: he was a great believer in the medical benefits of what was called 'air bathing'. He was also keen on practical experiments, and was one of a group of inventors who organized public demonstrations of electricity by spinning a glass ball against a leather pad to produce a build-up of static. As one contemporary put it: 'Franklin is a lightning rod philosopher who goes to the Charterhouse School each week, catches a charity boy, strings him up on silk cords, rubs him with glass and extracts sparks from his nose'. Franklin's other exploits included swimming in the Thames

ABOVE: *Benjamin Franklin – the US President who once swam on his back in the Thames while paring his nails – lived for a time in this fine Georgian house.*

at Chelsea on his back while paring his nails. He apparently did it merely to prove it could be done!

When his house in Craven Street was being restored, a mass of human bones was found buried in the basement. At first the police suspected a serial killer might have been at work there, but it turns out that Franklin lodged with one William Hewson, a doctor who ran an anatomy school from the house, and who would therefore have needed a regular supply of corpses. These would have been easy to come by, via the so-called Resurrection men, who stole bodies from graveyards; another source would have been the gallows that stood just behind the garden wall of No. 30, a few houses down.

While he lived at Craven Street, Franklin complained about the smoky fires in his rooms: the metal damper he invented to solve the problem is still there.

Gordon's Wine Bar
Headbangers' Hangout

At the bottom of Villiers Street, a short distance before Embankment Station, stands one of London's oddest bars. The entrance leads you into an empty area at the top of a staircase and it is only once you have descended that you realize quite what a strange place this is: Gordon's Wine Bar is probably the best place in London in which to bang your head continually.

The bar lies in the cellar of an old building, its ancient, brick-arched ceiling leaving barely enough headroom for the averagely tall, let alone six-footers. Gordon's is also one of the darkest bars in London: the cellar is lit only by candles, and it is easy to imagine a time when the Thames lapped just outside the walls on dark nights.

A wine bar has stood in this spot for centuries, and for much of the past 300 years Gordon's was run as a 'free vintner' – allowed to sell wine without a licence. By the 1970s, when many of the archaic licensing rules were changed, Gordon's was the last free vintner in London.

ABOVE: *Romance is not dead in Gordon's Wine Bar, where a candle-lit rendezvous is your only option, due to the hostelry's lack of electric light.*

York Watergate
His Lordship Doesn't Do Stairs

It is difficult to imagine now, but the easiest way to travel across London until comparatively recently was by water. For more than 1,000 years, the route from the City to Westminster or from one bankside warehouse to another was easiest by water: there were no traffic jams, no streets too muddy to pass and no tolls to be paid. Access to the river was via stairs that lined both shores until the building of the Embankment at the end of the 19th century. The very wealthy didn't have stairs, however: they had their palaces built right up against the river and built watergates so that their boats could glide in, saving them the indignity of having to hop out of a boat in full view of the public before climbing the stairs to their houses. Very few of these magnificent watergates survive. Perhaps the best is the York Gate, tucked away high and dry now in

Embankment Gardens. It looks as though it was put here so as to preserve it, but in fact the gate predates everything around it and lies in the position in which it was built when the river lapped against its stone steps.

York Watergate was built in 1626, when the Duke of Buckingham's great mansion was built here. In 1676 the mansion was demolished, but by some long-forgotten quirk of fate the watergate survived to be used by countless generations of watermen unloading passengers and cargo destined for the Strand. The

ABOVE: *York Watergate is now stranded in Victoria Embankment Gardens, but in times past the Thames flowed directly past the watergate's steps, which in turn led into the grand mansion of the Duke of York.*

gate was built either by Balthasar Gerbier, who was Surveyor to the Duke of Buckingham, or possibly by the great Classical architect Inigo Jones (1573–1652), who was Buckingham's protégé. Today it stands like an eccentric ghost more than 200 yards (220 metres) from the river it was built to serve.

Cleopatra's Needle
Under the Obelisk

Everything about Cleopatra's Needle is odd. For a start, it has nothing at all to do with the great Queen of Egypt. In common with many Egyptian artefacts its history is uncertain, but the most likely date for its creation is around 1500 BC. The needle was almost certainly commissioned by Thothmes III, whose name appears on the stone. By the year 23 BC it had been moved by Caesar to a position near Cleopatra's Palace. After that it vanishes from history until early in the 19th century, when it was presented by the local Egyptian ruler as a gift to King George IV. It arrived in London in 1878 after a long campaign to raise enough money to cover the cost of transporting it: the cost was huge, because the stone weighs a giant 160 tons, and a special case had to be made to avoid damaging it.

Once the obelisk arrived in England there was

BELOW: *The exact history of Cleopatra's Needle is uncertain, but when it was erected in London a mass of strange objects was buried beneath it.*

more trouble – a row started about where it should be erected. The forecourt of the British Museum was a popular choice; Kensington Gardens was another idea, as was Greenwich Park, but a site in Parliament Square near the House of Commons was finally decided on. To convince the doubters – of whom there were many – a wooden replica was built and erected in the square. Then disaster struck: the underground railway company whose line ran under the square was convinced that the obelisk would crash through the ground to the tunnel below. This argument was seen as compelling, and at last the obelisk was moved to its present position by the Thames – an appropriate enough location, given that it was first built to stand by the edge of the Nile.

If its journey to England was eccentric, the obelisk's final placing was even more so. The ancient tradition of burying either a child's shoe or a coin beneath a new building for good luck was here taken to ridiculous lengths. Among the objects buried beneath the obelisk (and still there) are: a model of the hydraulic equipment used to raise the obelisk; a two-foot rule; a child's feeding bottle and some toys; a tin of hairpins; some tobacco; a portrait of Queen Victoria; a map of London; a collection of newspapers; a set of coins; several empty jars; copies of the Bible; a translation of the hieroglyphics on the stone; a copy of Whittaker's Almanack; some rope; and some photographs of women.

The obelisk is a great survivor. Having come through the ravages of more than 3,000 years, it bears the marks of bomb damage from the Second World War. Londoners who grew fond of this oddity in their midst soon came up with a rhyme about it that manages to be both affectionate and dismissive:

'This monument as some supposes
Was put up in the time of Moses
It passed in time to the Greeks and Turks
But was put up here by the Board of Works.'

The Coal Hole
Singing in the Bath

Old pubs, though they have often been refurbished or even rebuilt, tend to survive longer than other buildings in the City of London – with the exception of churches, of course. The Coal Hole in Carting Lane is a case in point. The present building dates back to the early 1800s, but the pub commemorates an earlier nearby tavern of the same name. It gets its name from the wharf used by coalmen that stood nearby before the Embankment pushed the river further away. For centuries, coal was brought to London by ship from the mines of Northumberland and Durham, and the tough city coal heavers who lugged the sacks from ships up hill to the carters liked to drink in this pub.

During the 18th century the pub was hugely popular with actors and theatre managers, including the great tragedian Edmund Kean (1787–1833), who started a club called the Wolf Club. The sole qualification for membership was that the applicant should have been forbidden by his wife to sing in the bath! The Wolf Bar, in the present attractive Arts and Crafts interior with its pretty leaded windows, commemorates this bizarre drinking club. And when you step out of the pub you can still look down the sloping lane and see the bright river – just as the coal heavers of earlier centuries did.

The Savoy
Casting From the Rooftops

Two Americans staying in London once had an argument over whether or not it would be possible to cast a fly from the roof of their hotel – the Savoy – over the gardens and the busy Embankment and into the Thames.

So determined were they to settle the dispute that they went along to Hardy Brothers, the tackle makers, and asked them to decide if such a thing was possible. Hardy Brothers approached the angler and author Esmond Drury, who agreed to attempt the feat on condition that he was tied securely to a chimney on the hotel roof. Early one Sunday morning, and with the help of a policeman who stopped all the traffic on the Embankment, he proved that the feat was indeed possible!

The Savoy has always been a place that attracts eccentricity. Take the short street at the front, where taxis pull up to pick up hotel guests: this short stretch of road is the only place in the country where traffic is allowed to drive on the wrong side of the road.

The Savoy stands on the site of the old medieval

ABOVE: *The Coal Hole was the home of the Wolf Club, whose members were forbidden to sing in the bath.*

Savoy Palace, built by Henry III's friend Count Peter of Savoy in 1264. The courtyard at the front of the present hotel is said to follow the lines of the original medieval courtyard palace. The present building, completed in 1889, was built by Richard D'Oyly Carte, using the vast sums he made putting on Gilbert and Sullivan operas. The famous Peach Melba dessert was invented here (in honour of the great opera diva Nellie Melba), as was the dry Martini. And legend has it that if 13 guests find themselves about to sit down to supper, the hotel will provide a 14th guest (a black cat) to avert the bad luck supposedly inherent in the number 13.

There is also a long tradition that the hotel will put up with almost anything if the guest is important

ABOVE: *The Savoy Black Cat is the hotel's regular 14th guest, but visitors have in the past turned up with pet guests of their own, including crocodiles and monkeys.*

enough: one is alleged to have turned up with her pet crocodile, while others have appeared with monkeys, marmosets and parrots. The great violinist Jascha Heifetz (1899–1987) once took bagpipe lessons on the roof.

A little further west along the Strand from the Savoy is a short street that once ran down to the river. Savoy Street will take you to the Savoy Chapel, parts of which date back to the original foundation, which is contemporaneous with Count Peter's 12th-century palace. Most of the present building is relatively recent, but it was once the cause of a bizarre legal suit. Having reverted to the Crown following the death of Peter of Savoy, the chapel was given to the Duke of Lancaster – who also happened to be the king. This meant that the chapel was owned both by the king and by the Duke of Lancaster, but, as they were one and the same person, confusion reigned. The issue was only resolved in the early 18th century when the king sued the duke (i.e. he sued himself) to establish who had the right to the chapel

and the land on which it was built. Not surprisingly, the king won.

Rules
The Playful King

Horribly treated by his mother, Queen Victoria, the future Edward VII (1901–1910) let go of the reins entirely when the old queen finally died in 1901. The pious, serious son she had hoped to create by repeatedly telling him how hopeless he was in comparison to her late husband, had turned into a grossly overweight sensualist who enjoyed the favours of a string of mistresses and spent the relatively short time during which he was king indulging his passion for eating, drinking, shooting and, of course, womanizing.

No whiff of scandal was allowed to attach itself to the king of England, however, so elaborate efforts were made by the king's courtiers to enable him to do what he liked while appearing to stick to the rules of decorum and good behaviour. How did they do it? Well, at the 200-year-old Rules Restaurant in Maiden Lane they built a special side door that led to a private room where the king could entertain his mistresses, and when he went to the theatre he was ushered into a private, well-screened box far away from the public gaze.

Much of this is well known to us, but less well known is Edward VII's passion for fire engines – a passion that led to some very odd goings-on at No. 13 Rupert Street, Soho. Here, Edward would enter the premises as king and emerge disguised as a fireman sitting atop a fire engine. No one knows quite how often he indulged this passion, but it it was a habit that endured until within a few months of his death.

Macklin Memorial
Hot-headed

Memorials tend to celebrate the trade or profession of the deceased or their good deeds, although this is not always the case. Among the more bizarre of London's monuments is that to the Irish actor-manager Charles Macklin (1699–1797).

Macklin stepped onto the stage at Covent Garden when he was in his twenties, and for the next 70 years

ABOVE: *In Rules, the traditions of Edwardian dining have survived the test of time.*

BELOW: *The great 18th-century actor Charles Macklin designed his own grave memorial to remind others that he had once killed a man.*

he was rarely off it. His most celebrated role was that of Shylock in *The Merchant of Venice*, but he also played Othello and Macbeth in a legendary career.

Macklin was famously hot headed, endlessly getting into fights – often with his fellow actors. In 1735, he was drinking in the Green Room at Covent Garden when he fell into an argument; in the ensuing brawl the man was killed. Macklin escaped hanging on the grounds of self-defence, but he never forgot the trauma of the fight, and when he died aged 98 he left instructions that a memorial showing a skull pierced by a knife should be placed above his grave. That memorial can still be seen on the wall of one of London's most famous churches, St Paul's in Covent Garden.

Curiously, the church is the wrong way round. Churches were traditionally built with the altar at the east end and the entrance at the west. Under pressure from his patron the Duke of Bedford, the church's

architect Inigo Jones planned to have a grand entrance from the Covent Garden Piazza, but this meant placing the altar at the west end. Before the church could be consecrated – and despite the wealth and power of the duke – the church authorities intervened, and the east end of the church was blocked up to provide space for the altar. This explains the riddle of the dead-end grand portico that faces the piazza today.

Holborn & St Paul's

The area from Holborn to St Paul's has always had a somewhat forgotten air, but in many ways it epitomizes a city that has grown up organically, absorbing the oddities of individual eccentrics and developers, and accepting the fact that legislators are often determined to make things as delightfully complex as possible. Here, among other splendours, you will find a street that thinks it's in Cambridgeshire and a monument still blackened by the Great Fire of 1666.

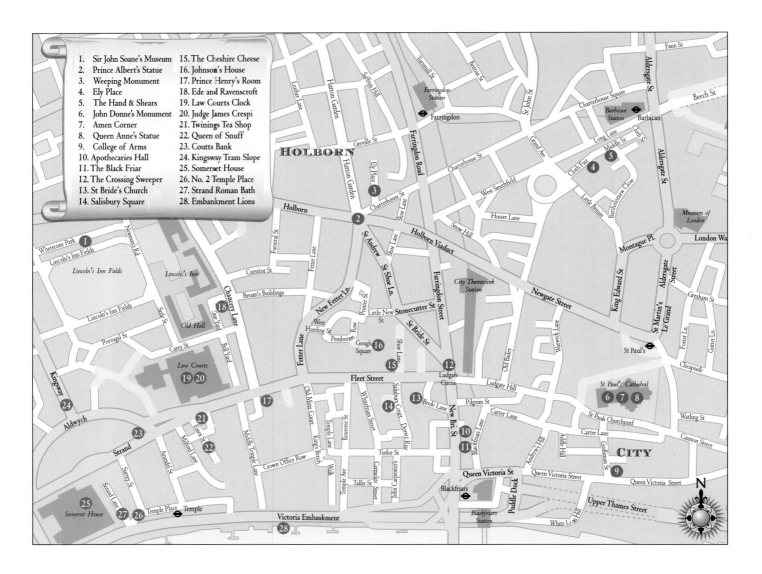

1. Sir John Soane's Museum
2. Prince Albert's Statue
3. Weeping Monument
4. Ely Place
5. The Hand & Shears
6. John Donne's Monument
7. Amen Corner
8. Queen Anne's Statue
9. College of Arms
10. Apothecaries Hall
11. The Black Friar
12. The Crossing Sweeper
13. St Bride's Church
14. Salisbury Square
15. The Cheshire Cheese
16. Johnson's House
17. Prince Henry's Room
18. Ede and Ravenscroft
19. Law Courts Clock
20. Judge James Crespi
21. Twinings Tea Shop
22. Queen of Snuff
23. Coutts Bank
24. Kingsway Tram Slope
25. Somerset House
26. No. 2 Temple Place
27. Strand Roman Bath
28. Embankment Lions

Black friars,
potty parrots and
full-bottomed wigs

Sir John Soane's Museum
A Passion for the Past

The English mania for collecting antiquities probably reached its apogee in Sir John Soane (1753–1837). Soane designed and built houses all over the country,

and most famously he designed the new Bank of England. In his private life, his passion for the past gradually forced him and his family to inhabit just two small rooms in the attic of their magnificent house in Lincoln's Inn Fields.

Soane's love of the relics of antiquity began early; in fact he is often seen as the father of the Classical revival in England. His collection first filled No. 13 Lincoln's Inn Fields, but as the house reached bursting point Soane was forced to use his skills as a designer and architect to create more space. He did it brilliantly, if eccentrically.

In the picture room, cunningly constructed panels line the walls, and each can be pulled out like the leaves of a book to reveal wonderful drawings and paintings within. The panels have the additional advantage of protecting the pictures – some of which are very rare and valuable – from the effects of too much exposure to light.

Eventually, Soane's collection took over the neighbouring houses – Nos 12 and 14 – and some idea of the vast scope of the collection can be gained from these statistics: the present-day museum contains 413 Greek and Roman marbles,

LEFT: *The Soane Museum, unchanged and unchanging, is the physical embodiment of its creator's dream.*

PREVIOUS PAGE: *Apothecaries Hall in the City of London is one of the area's least-altered ancient livery halls.*

ABOVE: *Albert doffs his hat to passers-by and reminds us that the crisp military salute is a relatively modern convention.*

including funerary urns, statues and friezes; 202 engraved seals; 59 Greek and Roman vases; 30 mummified cats and other curiosities; 266 water-colours; 1,420 Italian drawings; 8,044 drawings by Soane himself; 7,783 books and manuscripts; 34 models of antique buildings; 325 pieces of furniture; 8,856 drawings by James and Robert Adam; 166 medals; 104 pieces of stained glass; 68 oil paintings… the list goes on! The collection really does have to be seen to be believed!

Prince Albert's Statue
Hats Off!

The deference shown the Royal Family in Victorian times seems incomprehensible today. For 40 years after Albert's death from typhoid in 1861 (as a result of bad drainage at Windsor), statues and monuments to the great man popped up everywhere – often paid for, in fond memory, by people who could ill afford to pay. State-funded monuments, too, were erected at vast expense – most famously the great Albert Memorial in Kensington Gardens; and streets, stations, pubs and warehouses were named after him.

One statue has always baffled visitors to London. It is the statue of Albert as a field marshal in Holborn Circus. Albert was hardly the most warlike or militarily competent of royal consorts (he was actually a rather talented composer), yet there he sits astride a horse in his uniform, doffing his hat rather than saluting, as one might have expected. Saluting is a relatively modern and, some would say, rather vulgar gesture: until well into the Victorian era officers instead doffed their hats, just as Albert is doing here.

Weeping Monument
Cooke's Four

St Bartholomew the Great has several claims to fame. First, it is London's oldest church. Secondly – and most unusually – it was built by a court jester. Henry I's (1068–1135) fool, who was known as Rahere, had the church built in 1123, and went on to become its prior; he is buried here in the sanctuary.

ABOVE: *When the weather is right, there is a monument in the church of St Bartholomew the Great that weeps.*

ABOVE: *In many ways, Ely Place is a little piece of Cambridgeshire in a tiny corner of London.*

The building has escaped bombing, burning and even substantial rebuilding. There is less of it than there once was, certainly, for at the time of the Reformation it was trimmed down to its present size; in medieval times church buildings spread out across the present graveyard to Smithfield Market itself. The gateway into the church precincts was long hidden under plasterwork until early in the 20th century, when restorers discovered that it boasted fine Tudor craftsmanship, and it has now been restored.

Until recently, the so-called Butterworth charity was distributed every Good Friday on a table tomb in the churchyard: money and hot cross buns were handed out to the poor. Within the church endures an even stranger tradition. There is a bust of one Edward Cooke on the south wall. Cooke died in 1652, and the words carved in marble beneath his bust ask each passer-by to weep for him. If the passer-by finds he has no tears to spare, the inscription suggests he or she

should 'stay and see the marble weep'. And this really does happen: whether as a result of some divine intervention or, more prosaically, because of the bust's location in the church, condensation gathers in its smooth marble eyes and runs down in tear-like rivulets.

Ely Place
Beating the Bishop

One of the most interesting and unusual backwaters in London, Ely Place – just off High Holborn and a little above the course of the now-covered River Fleet – is easy to miss. It is one of the few places that still embodies the ancient rivalry between the Lord Mayor and the monarch, for within the City of London boundaries the mayor is in charge, and successive monarchs have had to accept this. They in turn have made sure that the mayor's jurisdiction is kept rigidly within the bounds of the old City limits. Traditionally, the monarch has to ask permission to enter the City, and this used to happen every year at a special ceremony at Temple Bar in the Strand.

Ely Place is within the City boundary and yet is owned by the Crown, and as such it is exempt from the authority of the Lord Mayor and remains a private road with its own gates and a beadle; even the police may enter this street only with the beadle's permission. Until about 1920 convention had it that a policeman had to be dispatched from the town of Ely, 100 miles away in Cambridgeshire, to police the street!

The history of this private enclave is long and unusual. Successive bishops of Ely had their London palace here from 1290 until 1772, when, neglected and almost in ruins, the palace was demolished. The palace had many famous residents over the years: John of Gaunt lived here from 1381 until his death in 1399. Henry VIII was an occasional visitor, as was his daughter Elizabeth I (1533–1603). One delightful story concerning Elizabeth is that she insisted that the Bishop of Ely rent some part of the palace to her courtier Sir Christopher Hatton, whose name is commemorated in the diamond-merchants' district of nearby Hatton Garden. The bishop was told he could charge Hatton 'ten pounds a year, ten loads of hay and a rose picked at midsummer.' In his play *Richard III*, Shakespeare mentions the wonderful strawberries that once grew in the gardens of the old palace.

The church of St Etheldreda, which is still here, was completed in about 1291 and is the oldest Roman Catholic pre-Reformation church in London – although 'church' is a rather grand name for what is effectively a small private chapel.

The houses that now surround St Etheldreda's were built at the end of the 18th century; until recently, Britain's only diamond cleaver carried on his business in one of them.

ABOVE: *The Hand & Shears, named for the ancient cloth fair that once took place here, was the scene of the Piepowder Sessions.*

The Hand & Shears
Cut Above the Rest

The bizarrely named Hand & Shears pub is a real curiosity. A clue about the origins of the name can be found in its address: it lies at Cloth Fair, where, as the name suggests, cloth sellers came with their goods from medieval times until the 1850s. The Hand & Shears got its name from the ancient tradition that opened the annual fair: the Lord Mayor would stop here on the appointed day and ceremonially cut a piece of cloth to signal that the fair was open.

LEFT: *The great metaphysical poet and churchman John Donne was incredibly well organized: he actually posed in his shroud for the monument that now stands in St Paul's Cathedral.*

Piepowder, whose name derives from the French *pied-poudreux*, meaning 'dusty-footed'. The merchants and their customers who came to the fair had travelled to get there and could be regarded as being dusty-footed: the court existed to settle disputes between them.

John Donne's Monument
Shrouded in Mystery

John Donne (1573–1631), author of some of the greatest short poems of the 17th century, is buried in St Paul's Cathedral, where he was dean for a number of years. Donne penned many famous lines, including 'No man is an island' and 'Ask not for whom the bell tolls: it tolls for thee'; but he was also a busy public man who sat as an MP in Elizabeth I's last parliament and worked for some time as a lawyer before taking holy orders. By the time he entered the Church he was already in middle age, but his piety only increased. Towards the end of his life he commissioned his own monument, a life-sized marble statue displaying the poet in his shroud, peeping gloomily from the folds of its hood.

Donne kept the monument in his house in the years leading up to his death, and when he died it was placed in old St Paul's. Nearly half a century later, in 1666, St Paul's burned down in the Great Fire and pretty much everything within it was destroyed – with one exception: John Donne's monument. Visitors can still observe the smoke-blackened lower parts of the marble, but Donne still peeps out intact from his hood. Even at the last the poet's wit did not desert him: he wrote his own epitaph, still visible today on the effigy: 'John Donne, Undone'.

The pub has an early 19th-century façade, but much of the interior is almost certainly a great deal older. The bars are small – one so much so that it is hard to get more than six people in it – and the old floors and matchboarded walls suggest earlier centuries. Certainly there has been a tavern here since the 16th century, and through the centuries in which the cloth fair was held, one of London's strangest courts met here regularly. This was the Court of

Amen Corner
Clergymen's Corner

There is a strange little street that curves back on itself just to the north of St Paul's Cathedral. It is lined with 17th- and 18th-century houses that were

built for the clergy who worked at the cathedral; several still have their original staircases and other features. The street in which they stand is always strangely quiet – far more so than one might imagine of a street in central London. This quietness owes itself to the high wall that runs along one side of the street, built to keep out the noise and in the inmates of Newgate Prison, which stood right next door. At the bottom of the wall, in one or two places, it is possible to see a few sections of the original medieval London wall, and beneath that layer it is believed that there are Roman courses of brickwork.

There is an attractive little garden here, too, together with three large water tanks: now used for plants and flowers, they were originally used to store water for the residents. A number of famous men have lived in Amen Corner, including, in the oldest remaining house, the essayist Sydney Smith (1771–1845). Smith was enormously intelligent, hugely popular and rather eccentric: it is said that he could have dined out three times a night, seven days a week, if he'd had the energy. As one contemporary put it, 'a light shines when he comes into a room'. Among Smith's most famous quips was: 'What a pity it is that we have only two amusements in England – vice and religion.'

Queen Anne's Statue
A Prisoner's Art

Visitors to London's great cathedral, St Paul's, will notice the rather worn statue of Queen Anne that stands directly in front of the main entrance facing down Ludgate Hill. This statue is unique in London, in that it was made by a convicted felon. Richard Belt, a Victorian sculptor, was commissioned to replace the original statue put up in 1712. The grime and rain of nearly two centuries had damaged it beyond repair, and Belt was a competent enough craftsman to create a copy. But what the authorities didn't know was that he was heavily in debt, and

RIGHT: *Queen Anne was allowed to stay put by Queen Victoria, fearful for the future of any statues of herself.*

ABOVE AND BELOW: *The College of Arms is, without a doubt, one of the crankiest places in London, but at least it gives heralds and pursuivants something to do.*

College of Arms
Better by Design

before the statue was complete he was sent to prison.

To save the embarrassment of having no statue to show for the money spent thus far on the work, the authorities secretly arranged for Belt to be allowed to complete the job in prison – and in so doing earn a little more toward paying off his debts.

The statue is also unique in London because it is the only statue that Queen Victoria (1819–1901) intervened to save. The courtiers planning her diamond jubilee in 1897 thought it would be easier to get the old lady to the church if they removed the statue, but Victoria was having none of it. She pointed out that if the authorities were prepared to move Queen Anne for her then they might well also be prepared subsequently to move a statue of her very self at the convenience of some future monarch.

The myriad mysteries wrapped in family coats of arms – their history, design, conception and meanings – can all be traced to an ancient, crooked, but still magnificent building in Queen Victoria Street.

A miraculous survivor of German bombs, the 17th-century College of Arms is home to the Royal heralds and to the kings at arms. There are three kings at arms: Garter, Norroy and Clarenceux. The royal heralds are York, Lancaster, Windsor, Chester, Somerset and Richmond. The college also houses the pursuivants – Rouge Dragon, Blue Mantle, Rouge Croix and Portcullis. In essence, all these officials simply help with royal and other state ceremonies. By tradition the head of the college – the Earl Marshall – is always the Duke of Norfolk, and to him falls the task of organizing State funerals, weddings and coronations.

The complex role of the holders of these titles would take a book in itself to explain!

More than five centuries after the college was established, no one, whether a company or an individual, is allowed to design and use a coat of arms without the permission of the college, and strict rules govern what may appear on any coat of arms; those who break the rules may be fined heavily for doing so.

The College of Arms still has in its possession charters relating to coats of arms and other documentation that survived the Great Fire of 1666, when the 15th-century building on this site was burned down. All the paperwork was bundled into a boat and taken to safety across the river.

Traditionally – though this is apparently not the case now – jobs in the college were given to important friends of important people, which may explain the long line of eccentrics who have snoozed away the decades in the ancient panelled rooms of this delightful building. Among the most eccentric was William Oldys (1696–1761), apparently given a job as a herald because England's foremost Duke, the Duke of Norfolk, had enjoyed reading Oldys's book about Sir Walter Raleigh. Oldys spent his days and evenings in a local pub but employed a man to carry him back to the college before midnight; any later and he would incur a fine. Oldys is best remembered today for a strange little poem he wrote towards the end of his life:

> Busy curious thirsty fly
> Drink with me and drink as I.
> Freely welcome to my cup
> Couldst thou sip and sip it up
> Make the most of life you may
> Life is short and wears away.

Apothecaries Hall
It's a Mystery

For more than three centuries, until the Reformation, the Black Friars – the biggest community of Dominicans in England – had their huge monastery

ABOVE: *The quiet courtyard at Apothecaries Hall was once surrounded by a guest house for the monks of the Black Friars order.*

between modern-day Ludgate and the river. Only a tiny fragment of the original building survives: a scrap of wall built into a later structure in Ireland Yard.

After the Dissolution in 1539, the monks' guest house became the Apothecaries Hall, and the apothecaries are still there today. Their original building was burned down in the Great Fire, but much of the building that replaced it in 1688 survives today, while the vast majority of guildhalls have either gone or been rebuilt. This is the oldest livery hall in London, situated around a quiet courtyard and down a narrow lane, and giving the visitor a real sense of what medieval London must have been like.

A few changes were made in the 18th century and then again in the 1920s, but the hall still has its massive, beautifully made 17th-century staircase, and

ABOVE: *The Black Friar is a monument to the Art Nouveau movement, and is the City's only pub in this architectural style.*

the great hall, courtroom and panelled parlour are also unchanged. Among other curiosities are a magnificent 18th-century candelabrum and a portrait bust of Gideon de Launce, an apothecary who died in 1659 having fathered some 39 children!

The apothecaries were in general a curious lot, and were forever bringing lawsuits against the Company of Surgeons, each side arguing over areas of jurisdiction. The area of expertise they now cover was agreed in 1723 after months of wrangling in front of the Law Lords. Today the apothecaries are one of only a few livery companies that still grant qualifications to practise their 'mystery', as a trade was called in medieval times.

The Black Friar
Masses of Mosaics

At the northern end of Blackfriars Bridge – itself a splendid creation of the mid-Victorian era – stands a

bizarre and unique London pub. As is the case with many streets and alleyways in this historic part of London, the pub's name commemorates an ancient Dominican monastic foundation that existed on the banks of the Thames until the Reformation.

The pub has a wonderful life-size statue of a black friar high above the front door, but what really makes the place so special is that it is London's only Art Nouveau pub. It has survived remarkably intact since 1909, when the original first-floor interior was altered by H. Fuller Clark. The bars are filled with bronze figures of monks, and lined with costly multi-coloured marble. Externally the pub is equally eccentric, with masses of mosaics and carved figures by Henry Poole.

The Crossing Sweeper
A Clean Sweep

The trade of the crossing sweeper – who cleared horse droppings from the streets – vanished, of course, with the coming of the motor car. Perhaps history's most famous crossing sweeper was a fictional one – Jo in Charles Dickens's novel *Bleak House*. Illiterate, half-

ABOVE: *Copper monks, rather than black friars, line the walls inside The Black Friar, reminding us that religious houses were once centres of brewing and drinking.*

dressed even in winter and forced to sleep in the streets, Jo earns a few pennies each day by sweeping a path through the horse manure from one side of a London street to another – poverty, malnutrition and cold eventually lead to his death. Many destitute men, women and children were forced into this work simply because they had nothing else, and one real-life crossing sweeper, with a remarkable story, was Brutus Billy, also known as Charles McGhee.

Nothing is known of McGhee's history, but he was an elderly black man who had probably come to England from the West Indies. He may have been a slave at one time. For many years in the early 19th century he swept a path across Fleet Street where it meets Ludgate Hill, near a wealthy linen draper's shop. The shop was owned by Robert Waithman, who later became MP for the City of London. From the window above the shop, the draper's daughter watched the old crossing sweeper, and on cold days she would arrange for someone to take him a bowl of hot soup and some bread.

When McGhee died some years later, it was discovered that he had left all his savings – some £700, which was an extraordinary sum in Victorian times – to this kind girl.

St Bride's Church
Let Them Eat Cake

The design for the traditional wedding cake – several tiers of cake covered with icing – has its origins in a church just behind Fleet Street – a church that, equally curiously, happens to be called St Bride's.

St Bride, or Bridget, was once one of England's most popular saints, not least because she had reputedly been able to transform water into beer. The association of her church with the wedding cake stems from the entrepreneurial spirit of a Fleet Street baker who lived at the end of the 18th century. An expert cake maker, Mr Rich was always on the look-out for new lines and designs. Gazing across the street towards St Brides one day, he wondered if it would be possible to reproduce the church's elaborate spire in icing sugar. After a few failed attempts he succeeded, and the resulting cake became hugely popular and made him rich.

St Bride's Church replaces a much earlier building: in fact, archaeologists tell us that there were at least

seven churches on this site before Sir Christopher Wren (1632–1723) designed the building we see today. Two monuments add to the church's delightful eccentricity: the first is a small plaque that is easily missed. It carries the name of Virginia Dare, the first English child to be born in the United States. The other is to Wren:

Clever men like Christopher Wren
Only occur just now and then
No, never a cleverer dipped his pen
Than clever Sir Christopher, Christopher Wren.

Salisbury Square
Book Burning

Salisbury Square, just off Fleet Street, witnessed the conclusion to one of the wackiest legal disputes in the history of England. The problem began when the Duke of York began to lose interest in one of his mistresses, one Mrs Clarke. Mrs Clarke was aggrieved that the duke no longer wanted her, but she would have accepted her fate meekly enough had the duke given her the pension she felt she deserved, together with a house in a fashionable part of London. The duke, for his part, thought that he could simply discard her and that would be the end of it; he had not anticipated the fury of a woman scorned.

When the duke refused to see her or give her any money, Mrs Clarke sat down and wrote her memoirs – in particular her memories of her relationship with the duke. The notoriety of Mrs Clarke and the public's appetite for scandal meant that the publisher was convinced he would achieve huge sales and make his fortune, so he printed no fewer than 10,000 copies – an enormous print-run for any book at that time. Mrs Clarke let the duke know that the book was about to come out, whereupon he immediately produced the money for her pension, bought her a house and bought up all 10,000 copies of the book – which were ceremoniously piled up in Salisbury Square and burned. Were one copy to have survived and were to turn up now, it would no doubt be worth a fortune!

LEFT: *A humble cake maker was inspired by Sir Christopher Wren's spire on St Bride's Church and, as a result, created a tradition that continues today.*

Ye Olde Cheshire Cheese
Polly the Parrot

The Great Fire of London destroyed Old St Paul's, crept down Ludgate Hill towards the River Fleet and even engulfed a number of houses on the west of the river in what is today Fleet Street.

Fleet Street was always famously bordered by a mass of tangled courts and alleyways typical of a crowded city that had grown slowly over many centuries. Most of these courtyards and alleys are now built over or lined with dull office buildings, but in Wine Office Court there is a surprising survivor – a late 17th-century pub that looks exactly inside as it would have looked when it was first built. What's more, the interior is not a re-creation: the tables in the public bar, the fireplace, the décor and the pictures on the wall have for the most part been here for at least 200 years.

The fame of the Cheshire Cheese spread far and wide, and from the 1850s it was on the itinerary of most visitors to London. By 1900, the pub had a resident who was to become almost as famous as the Cheese itself: Polly the Eccentric Parrot. Famously garrulous and rude about visitors she didn't like, Polly celebrated the end of the First World War in 1918 in her inimitable way, mimicking the noise of popping champagne corks some 400 times before falling off her perch, suffering from exhaustion. When she died in 1926, Polly was thought to be over 40 years old, and her antics over the years earned her an accolade unequalled in the animal kingdom: her obituary appeared in more than 200 newspapers worldwide.

Polly lived at the Cheese during its most famous days, and the list of celebrities who drank here is extraordinary. Literary figures are for the most part associated with the pub: Dr Johnson (1709–84), who lived just two minutes' walk away in Gough Square, is reported to have come here every night for years along with his friend and biographer James Boswell (1740–95); Charles Dickens sat through many a long evening in the corner by the door in the room

ABOVE RIGHT AND RIGHT: *Ye Olde Cheshire Cheese not only once housed a most eccentric parrot, it also welcomed a host of literary figures to its bar, including the 19th-century novelist Wilkie Collins.*

from Theodore Roosevelt (1858–1919) to Mark Twain (1835–1910) and Sir Arthur Conan Doyle (1859–1930) came here.

Above the fireplace in the public bar is a fascinating portrait, dating from 1829 and darkened by the smoke of countless candles and coal fires, of the waiter William Simpson. The picture is interesting not only because paintings of servants are rare, but because the very table on which Simpson leans in his portrait still stands in the bar nearby.

In the 19th century the Cheese had one other claim to eccentricity: its landlord made some of the biggest pies in London. Filled with beef, oysters and lark, each pie weighed 50–80lbs (23–36kg), and was big enough to feed some 100 people! Among those who ceremonially dined on the first serving were Conan Doyle and Prime Minister Stanley Baldwin (1867–1947).

ABOVE AND BELOW: *Dr Johnson's House is a miraculous survival amid the redevelopment of Fleet Street, and is a monument to one of the capital's great eccentrics.*

opposite the public bar; in the 18th century the actor and impresario David Garrick came here with his friends, the painter Sir Joshua Reynolds (1723–92) and Edward Gibbon (1737–94), author of *The Decline and Fall of the Roman Empire*; novelist Wilkie Collins (1824–89) was a regular, together with Alfred, Lord Tennyson (1809–92) and the social historian Thomas Carlyle (1795–1881); in the 20th century, everyone

Dr Johnson's House
Mad About Words

Gough Square, just off the north side of Fleet Street, is easy to miss. To get to it you have to walk through a narrow alley barely wide enough for two men to pass. The square has been redeveloped several times over the centuries, but standing high and dry and almost in the middle of it is a tall, thin house unchanged externally since the late 17th century, and internally just as it was when the great Dr Johnson lived here in the middle years of the 18th century.

Johnson was one of London's great eccentrics: despite his formidable intelligence he was prone to fits of rage followed by bouts of melancholy; his shambling, absent-minded way of walking attracted the attention of passers-by, who often assumed he was a madman or a tramp; wherever he walked he talked continually to himself, twitching and shaking his head from morning till night whether he had company or not.

It was in the attic of this beautifully preserved house (which is little

ABOVE: *Little-known and rarely visited, Prince Henry's Room dates from before the Great Fire of London in 1666.*

Prince Henry's Room
It's the Real Thing

visited despite the fame of its greatest tenant) that Johnson spent more than a decade working seven days a week and often late into the night to complete – almost single-handedly – the first dictionary of the English language.

In the parlour Johnson would have entertained many of his friends, including the writer Oliver Goldsmith, actor and impresario David Garrick and, of course, his biographer the great James Boswell, who immortalized the great man's sayings. Hidden away amid the reams of serious poetry and prose are some decidedly eccentric poetic efforts: following his death, among the great lexicographer's effects was found the following verse, carefully copied out:

> I put my hat upon my head
> And walked into the Strand
> And there I met another man
> Whose hat was in his hand.

The house was threatened with demolition early in the 20th century, and it was the intervention of no less a figure than Lord Harmsworth – then owner of the *Daily Mail* newspaper – that saved it.

At the bottom of Chancery Lane, where it meets Fleet Street there are several old houses – one or two of them among the oldest still standing in London, though their external restorations and alterations make it difficult to tell. No. 17 Fleet Street is the real thing: a genuine pre-Great Fire house, surviving largely intact. The Great Fire crept up Fleet Street almost as far as this house, but thankfully halted a few houses to the east.

There has, in fact, been a house here since the 12th century; at one time it was owned by the Knights of St John of Jerusalem before becoming an inn called The Hand. Then, in 1610, records show that the inn was largely rebuilt and its name changed to The Prince's Arms. It was at this time that the main room above the gateway was completed, with its beautiful plaster ceiling and fine oak panelling. The dominant motif on the plasterwork and elsewhere is of the three Prince of Wales feathers together with the letters 'PH'. The design was probably made in honour of James I's son Prince Henry, who became Prince of Wales in 1610. How this extraordinary room survived the next few hundred years when so many other early buildings were demolished or changed out of all recognition is a mystery, and one to rejoice at.

ABOVE: *If you're in urgent need of a custom-made full-bottomed wig, then there's only one place to go: Ede and Ravenscroft in Chancery Lane.*

Ede and Ravenscroft
Keep Your Hair On!

Throughout the 17th century and much of the 18th, no self-respecting gentleman would have dreamt of stepping outside his house without his wig. Wigs were simply a part of elegant dress, as essential to the man of fashion as a jacket is to a modern suit. By the 19th century, though, wigs had all but disappeared – except among the legal profession, where the tradition still holds fast.

The traditions and techniques involved in making a legal wig are much as they were for any 17th-century wig, and one wig-making firm survives to this day using the old methods. Ede and Ravenscroft can trace their origins, as robe-makers, to 1689. Then, in 1726, Thomas Ravenscroft, a wig-maker from Shropshire, moved to London and began making wigs for the Church and the legal profession. His grandson Humphrey invented the legal wigs we know today, known as 'forensic' wigs. Though similar in essence to earlier wigs, the forensic wig did not need to be constantly curled and dusted.

Originally, Ravenscroft traded in Serle Street, London, but in the 1890s a daughter of the firm, Rosa, married Joseph Ede, the son of a well-known robe-maker, and the modern firm was born. It took premises at No. 93 Chancery Lane, in the heart of London's legal district, where it can still be found.

Each wig is individually made to order, using only horsehair. The firm makes some 1,000 barristers' wigs a year, about 120 bench wigs (a judge's working wig) and around 100 full-bottomed wigs, which are worn at ceremonial occasions and only by judges. Each one is made on a wooden head-shaped block. Homeworkers weave the horsehair, which is then stitched onto a silk netting base, with neat, tight curls and no gaps; all the horsehair is curled using old-fashioned curling tongs, which are heated on a fire. It takes three or four weeks to make a barrister's wig and about 24 hours to weave enough horsehair for just one wig, and the result is said to last a lifetime.

The quaint old shopfront in Chancery Lane also reveals that the company makes coronation robes – in fact, it has made every British coronation robe since 1689.

Law Courts' Clock
Striking the Hours

London is a great place for public clocks, and although remarkably accurate clocks and watches are now cheap to buy, it was not always thus. Public and church clocks were vital in an age when they were the only means for the majority of the population to tell the time.

Henry VIII was responsible for passing a law that stated that all church and other official clocks in London must be painted blue and gold; they also typically had a bell or chime, so that those who were hurrying to work would know whether they needed to speed up when they heard the distant sound of a clock striking the hours or the quarters.

London has numerous eccentric clocks: the clock at St Dunstan's in the West, with its giants beating the hours on a bell with their clubs; or the modern clock with elaborate figures and bells outside the Swiss Centre in Leicester Square; and there is Fortnum and Mason's historic clock out- side their famous shop depicting the shop's founders. But perhaps the most intriguing and least known is the law courts' clock.

What makes this clock so unusual is that it was built by an illiterate Irishman who made clocks only as a hobby; and yet it is supremely accurate: in fact, when complet- ed, it was said to be the most accurate clock in London. A difficulty arose when a second clock was needed and the court authorities wanted something of similar quality. Only then was it discovered that the original had been made by a man who, because he could not write, had kept no record of how he made it – which is why the law courts' clock is unique and always will be!

ABOVE: *The Law Courts' Clock is a beautifully made and highly accurate timepiece, yet curiously no records exist about how it was made.*

Judge James Crespi
Fleet Street Giant

Caesar James Crespi was born in 1928 and educated at Cambridge. He was a remarkable eccentric by any standards, although by profession he became a quite brilliant advocate. He claimed that he saved his most eloquent speeches for the Fleet Street wine bar El Vinos, where the wine waiter apparently always greeted him with a clenched fist across his breast and the words 'Ave, Mr Crespi'. He also became enormously fat, though luckily all the taxi drivers knew him by sight so he never walked anywhere; his huge bulk made it virtually impossible for him to walk, anyway. One novice cabby, though, is said once to have mistaken Crespi's wing collar for the dress of a waiter, and dropped him at the staff entrance to the Savoy.

Crespi married a woman he met in a nightclub, but for reasons he was never able to recall; he described the marriage as 'obviously a case of mistaken identity', and it lasted less than a week. When asked if he regretted anything in life he simply said, 'Being mistaken for Lord Goodman, whoever he is'.

Twinings Tea Shop
A Sinful Drink

Twinings Tea Shop in Fleet Street is the oldest such establishment in Britain, a survivor of war, redevelopment and changes in fashion. In short, Twinings is a sort of commercial ghost from the 18th century.

The business has been run by 10 consecutive Mr Twinings, each the son of the last. The shop – which had previously been known as Tom's Coffee House – was opened here by Thomas Twining, a weaver from Gloucestershire, in 1702, and though there are older shops in London, none has continually occupied the same site for so long.

The shop's frontage is tiny, though when it first opened London would have been full of similarly diminutive shops.

Christopher Wren and Samuel Johnson bought their tea here, as did Queen Anne (1665–1714), actor David Garrick (1717–79), Irish novelist Oliver Goldsmith (1728–74) and any number of famous 18th-century figures. Above the shop front are two beautiful alabaster figures, put up in the 1780s.

At the end of the 18th century, tea was very heavily taxed. In 1706, for example, a ¼lb (100g) of Twinings Gunpowder Green Tea cost (in modern terms) £160! Tea was seen as a luxury, much loved by the wealthy but out of the reach of the poor – all because the government

ABOVE: *The figure that sits above Twinings' shopfront is a remnant of a time when symbols rather than words were used by merchants to advertise their wares.*

BELOW: *To step into Twinings Tea Shop is like entering a timewarp, and there is a fragrant range of rare and exotic teas mixed by experts.*

ABOVE: *In the 18th century, tea was heavily taxed, and Twinings were selling their Gunpowder Green Tea for a hefty £160 per ¼lb (100g).*

insisted on placing such a heavy excise duty on it. The result, though, was not increased revenue for the State's coffers but rather a huge increase in smuggling. According to one story, the tax was only reduced when Prime Minister William Pitt the Younger (1759–1806) asked Mr Twining his advice. Twining told the PM to reduce the tax on tea to a tenth of its current level; the smuggling would all but stop, and the vast increase in legitimate sales would actually increase government revenues. Pitt took Twining's advice, and the tea merchant was proved right: government revenues soared, and tea drinking became the passion of every class of British society. As with anything new, the Church was outraged: tea drinking was sinful, said the bishops!

Today the long, narrow shop still sells a range of teas; old portraits adorn the walls, and at the back there is a museum filled with artefacts from the three-centuries-old business.

Queen of Snuff
A Snuff Addict in the Strand

When she made her will in the early part of the 19th century, Mrs Margaret Thomson, who lived in Essex Street, just off the Strand, stipulated that her coffin be filled with all the snuff handkerchiefs that were unwashed at the time of her death; she also wanted to be surrounded with snuff in her coffin. Six of the greatest snuff-takers in the parish were requested to be her pall-bearers, and each was asked to wear a snuff-coloured hat. Six girls were instructed to walk behind the hearse, each with a box of snuff – which they were to take copiously for their refreshment as they went along.

Mrs Thomson left the priest who officiated at the ceremony five guineas on condition that he partook of snuff during and throughout the funeral proceedings. And in return for a bequest of snuff, her servants were instructed to walk in front of the funeral procession throwing snuff on the ground and onto the crowd of onlookers. Throughout the long day of the funeral, snuff was distributed to all those attending.

ABOVE: *A statue of Thomas Coutts, one of the founders of the bank that now serves the Queen, graces the bank's refurbished central atrium.*

Coutts Bank
Let's All Go Down the Strand

Coutts Bank is one of the oldest and most prestigious in the world. The firm has been in the Strand since 1692, and in its present office at No. 440 since 1904, when it moved to make way for Charing Cross Station. Until the 1970s, all Coutts staff were required to wear frock coats, and the only pens available to customers were Victorian ink pens. All Coutts cheques once bore a detailed description of the bank's original location: 'At the Sign of the Three Crowns in the Strand next Door to the Globe Tavern'.

Much of this delightful eccentricity vanished when the bank was taken over by a much bigger firm, but Coutts are still bankers to the Royal Family, and the entrance to their Strand branch is still guarded by two men in frock coats. The Coutts Director's Room is still hung with the hand-made Chinese wallpaper given to Thomas Coutts in the 18th century, said to be among the first Chinese wallpapers to reach Europe; such was its value that when the bank moved from its previous Strand address, the wallpaper was carefully removed and rehung – in a room that had to be built to precisely the same dimensions as the old one. When, in the 1970s, the whole block of which Coutts formed a part was redeveloped (leaving the Nash façade) the whole process was repeated so as to preserve the wallpaper. Coutts's archive today includes the clothes worn by the first Mr Coutts, and all Queen Victoria's bank books.

Kingsway Tram Slope
Still on Track

Those lovely old trams that ran across London in the first part of the 20th century vanished as soon as motor buses were generally available, and most people presume that not a trace of their former presence remains, but one section of tramline is in fact still extant.

Go along High Holborn until you reach Kingsway, a thoroughfare built as part of the Aldwych redevelopment and which destroyed a vast warren of tiny streets and lanes lined with 15th- and 16th-century timber-framed houses. Turn right onto Kingsway, and you will immediately notice a long rectangle enclosed by railings in the middle of the road. Brave the traffic to peer through the railings, and you will see tramlines descending a slope. This tram slope was once the underground entrance to a tram depot, and though the trams disappeared more than half a century ago, the lines and the cobbles through which they ran remain to this day.

Somerset House
Palace of Varieties

When the Inland Revenue moved out of the last great palace on the Strand – 18th-century Somerset House – a beautiful and little-known building was at last made visible to a wider public. The vast, quiet court-yard is no longer a dreary car park, it instead boasts fountains and restaurants and even, in winter, an ice rink. There is also access to the great gravel terrace that once looked directly out over the river (and now looks out first over the Embankment to the river beyond).

Somerset House, which dates back to 1775, was built for Lord Protector Somerset after the Reformation. George III (1738–1820) commissioned the architect William Chambers to build something that would house the various arts societies of which the king was patron (these included the Royal Academy and the Society of Antiquaries), as well as burgeoning government departments. Although the Royal Academy moved long ago to its present home in Piccadilly, the Courtauld Institute is still based here.

ABOVE: *Kingsway Tram Slope in the very centre of London is one of the last places where traces of the capital's former transport system can still be seen.*

What makes this splendid building bizarre is the old cellar known as the Dead Room. The story begins with Charles I. Too shrewd to make his feelings public, Charles secretly sympathized with the Roman Catholic faith. He knew he could not be King of England if he proclaimed his Catholicism, so he waited until he was on his deathbed to pronounce his adherence to the old religion.

His French wife Henrietta Maria, who had never claimed to be anything other than Catholic, was now a widow with nowhere to live. She moved to

ABOVE: *Somerset House may have seen several rounds of rebuilding, yet a secret graveyard has managed to survive in the Dead Room cellar.*

Somerset House along with her vast retinue of servants – all French and all devoutly Catholic. As they grew old and died, these Catholics presented the authorities with a huge problem: because of their faith no churchyard or burial ground in London would have anything to do with them, so a graveyard was created in the grounds of the house. Though they have been disturbed by various bouts of rebuilding, at least five graves still lie deep in the new building, their memorial stones fixed to the wall of the 'Dead Room' cellar.

Strand Roman Bath
Window on the Past

In Strand Lane, just off the Strand, one may glimpse a very odd antiquity. Though it is always referred to as Roman, this curious red-brick bath actually has far more mysterious origins. The truth is that no one knows how old it is: it was certainly here in the 17th century, and may be much older, but professional archaeologists have thrown doubt on claims that it is Roman – though not conclusively.

The bath certainly appears to be made of small, typically Roman red bricks, but it is curious that there is no mention of it in the records until the 17th century. Although now dry, the bath – measuring almost 16 feet by 8 feet (5 by 2.5 metres) – was once fed by a holy well, a nearby natural spring long since diverted into a pipe. Sadly, you can only see it by going down a narrow alley and peering through a small (usually murky) window.

No. 2 Temple Place
Office Antics

No. 2 Temple Place, just behind the Embankment near Waterloo Bridge, is one of the most extraordinarily luxurious offices in London. It was built in Portland stone in 1895 by the fabulously wealthy American millionaire William Waldorf Astor. Astor employed John Loughborough Pearson as his architect, but was absolutely rigid in his insistence that certain types of wood and marble be used and that only the finest craftsmen should be employed for every detail of the work. Virtually every part of the interior – from the ebony columns to the marble and stonework and even the window grilles – was handmade. The cost was astronomical – certainly tens of millions of pounds in today's terms. Yet the money and effort were expended not to produce a fabulous home but merely an office for just one man!

Astor had a copper model of the *Santa Maria* – the ship in which Columbus sailed to America – fixed to a weathervane on the roof and in the courtyard there are two cherubs, each holding a telephone receiver!

Embankment Lions
Always be Prepared

Before the Thames Barrier was built in the early 1980s, London was in constant danger of flooding. Despite the considerable height of the Embankment walls, nothing could control the great surges that occasionally began far out at sea and then drove remorselessly upriver. When heavy rain in winter coincided with a big spring tide, the Embankment was often breached in numerous places, causing tens of thousands of pounds-worth of damage to property, not to mention disruption to transport and people's lives generally. A bizarre early-warning system did exist, however, and it is still partially in use today.

ABOVE: *The magnificent lions' heads along the Embankment are not just decorative, they also act as an early flood-warning system.*

Well below the parapet wall of the Embankment, and fixed at regular intervals, are bronze casts of lions' heads with what look like mooring rings hanging from their mouths, although the passengers of any boat tying up at one of these rings could not possibly disembark. But these rings are not for mooring, rather every policeman whose beat takes him along the Embankment on either side of the river is instructed to keep an eye on the lions' heads because if the water level reaches the heads flooding is a serious and imminent danger.

West & South-west London

If you know where to look, the south and south-west of London are rich in quirky survivals and historic oddities. For natural history lovers there is an extraordinary artificial wetland, while for pottery enthusiasts there is an 18th-century bottle kiln hidden away in Fulham. And while the Army are forbidden to march in one place, in another pirates can be found.

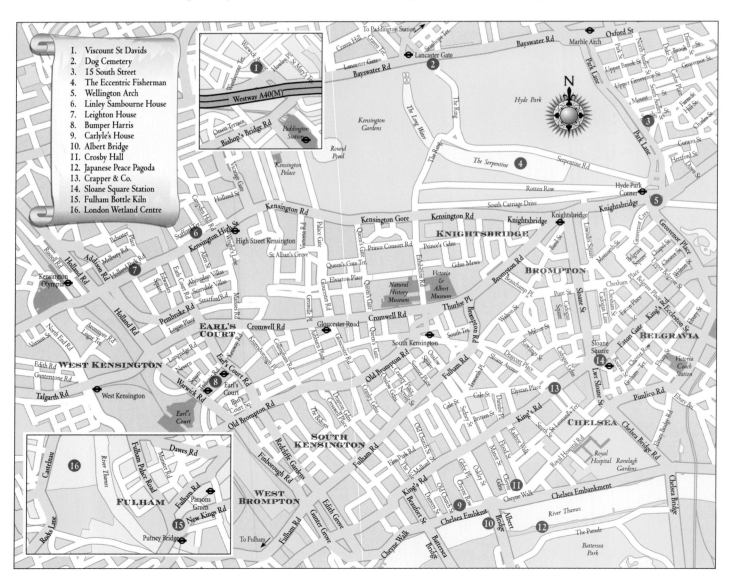

1. Viscount St Davids
2. Dog Cemetery
3. 15 South Street
4. The Eccentric Fisherman
5. Wellington Arch
6. Linley Sambourne House
7. Leighton House
8. Bumper Harris
9. Carlyle's House
10. Albert Bridge
11. Crosby Hall
12. Japanese Peace Pagoda
13. Crapper & Co.
14. Sloane Square Station
15. Fulham Bottle Kiln
16. London Wetland Centre

From Peg Leg to Punch and rampant horses to Arabian nights

Viscount St Davids
The Pirate King

Viscount St Davids, Jestyn Reginald Austin Plantagenet Phillips, was the second Viscount St Davids. He was born in 1917 and educated at Eton; he married three times, and for a while worked as a mate on a sailing barge. His father was already a baronet, the head of an ancient family in South Wales and a direct descendant of a 12th-century knight crusader, but our eccentric viscount set up a company to run barge trips on the Regent's Canal in London. He quickly went bust, and two years later vanished without trace after leaving his home and second wife, ostensibly to buy a newspaper; in fact he set sail for the West Indies as a deckhand on a merchant ship.

St Davids succeeded to the viscountcy in 1938, and was eventually to sit in the House of Lords alongside his mother, who was Baroness Strange of Knokin, Hungerford and De Moleys. He

PREVIOUS PAGE: Wellington Arch: grand, imposing and once the scene of a bizarre dinner party.

BELOW: Viscount St Davids, or Peg Leg as he was known, was one of London's most endearing eccentrics.

spoke only rarely in the House, and on rather off-beat issues: the sale of fireworks and the legality of the American practice of trick-or-treating were two of his favourite subjects.

Famously eccentric, St Davids bought a copy of *The Times* every day but never read it: instead he used it to build embankments and mountains for his model railway. His other great interest was boats, and he spent many years living on a barge on the Grand Union Canal at Paddington. He was known to local children as Peg Leg or the Pirate King because he had a pronounced limp and lacked several of his front teeth. He founded the Pirate Club in Camden, which gave poor children the chance to mess about in boats. He died in 1991.

Dog Cemetery
Animal Magic

When the Duke of Cambridge's (1819–1904) much-loved dog was run over by a carriage outside the Victorian lodge on the north-east side of

Hyde Park, the poor animal was carried to the lodge, where it expired. The duke was at that time head ranger of both Hyde Park and St James's. Clearly a man of some influence, he asked that the dog be buried behind the lodge, and in doing so he began a tradition that lasted from 1880, when the Duke's dog as buried, until the 1950s. In that time more than 200 dogs, cats, parrots, geese and at least one monkey were buried here, each with its own beautifully carved headstone; in several cases grieving owners visited the site of the graves for decades after their beloved animals had departed.

15 South Street
Didn't Give a Fig!

One of the most eccentric women of the 19th century, Catherine Walters is also proof that the power of personality can overcome almost any obstacle.

She was known to all as Skittles, and was a great beauty – as well as being the last in a line of professional courtesans stretching back to before Nell Gwynn. It is remarkable that she lived in the way that she did during an age that was probably the most moralistic – even if hypocritically so – in history. The Victorian obsession with purity and chastity outside marriage, combined with the absolute rule of respectability, meant that any middle- or working-class woman suspected of sexual 'irregularity' (as the Victorian newspapers might have put it) would be shunned by everyone; but, as always, there was one rule for the majority and an entirely different rule for the elite.

Because Mrs Walters was the paid mistress of a number of members of the aristocracy and royalty, she had to be received into society if her various partners insisted on it.

Yet even without her aristocratic patronage, the decidedly eccentric Skittles would no doubt have

BELOW: *Tucked away in Hyde Park is a Dog Cemetery founded by the Victorians, who were hugely sentimental about their pets.*

ABOVE: *Catherine Walters, also known as Skittles, was an aristocratic courtesan who managed to achieve respectability.*

The Eccentric Fisherman
Writing it All Down

Until relatively recently, the Knightsbridge corner of the Serpentine Lake in London's Hyde Park offered urban youngsters the chance to fish. All that was required to fish this lake and a dozen others in different London parks was a letter to the Parks Superintendent requesting permission, so every year the letters flowed in from schoolchildren across the capital. One or two adults had always requested permits too, and among these was one extraordinary man. He was probably in his sixties, very tall and very thin, and he always fished using the longest rod anyone had ever seen. He didn't bother with the other parks – Hyde Park and its Knightsbridge corner were enough for him. But he only fished one day a week, always on a Saturday, and he always fished from the same park bench. For as long as anyone could remember, he had never missed a Saturday in any season.

But it wasn't only these regular habits that made our fisherman so eccentric. He used an old-fashioned hollow-cane roach pole – a piece of equipment much loved by elderly cockneys – of enormous length, fitted with a huge antique reel.

Youngsters who were new to the Knightsbridge corner would secretly laugh at the thin man with the roach pole – though only until a more experienced boy pointed out that though the thin man might look odd, he was extraordinarily good at fishing. In fact, for the boys who fished the Knightsbridge corner regularly, the thin man was something of a hero. While they might catch a few fish, even a dozen on a good day, the thin fisherman might easily catch 40 or 50, and his were almost always bigger than anyone else's.

His technique, like everything else about him, was unusual. He never used maggots, which were almost universally used by other anglers; he never hurried; and he never showed the least sign of excitement when he hooked and landed a specimen that had every other angler gazing at him open-mouthed.

While the boys were delighted if they caught tiddlers, the thin man always seemed able to find the bright gold – and much coveted – crucian carp. On one memorable day he caught a dozen beauties, all over 2lbs (1kg), before topping his success with the

survived anyway. She was in many respects immune to the rules that applied to most people simply because she didn't give a fig about them. She was the mistress of the Duke of Devonshire and the Marquis of Hartington, among others, and insisted on the finest clothes and carriages – finer even, it was said, than the wives of her lovers. Stories about her are legion. She loved riding, and when hunting with the Quorn in Leicestershire she once famously kept up with the leaders of the field until the fox was caught; the master of hounds ventured to compliment her on the flushed colour of her cheeks: 'That's nothing', she allegedly replied. 'You should see the colour of my ruddy arse!'

Skittles lived for many years at 15 South Street in Mayfair – the house is still there – and in old age was pushed in her wheelchair through Hyde Park by none other than the statesman Lord Kitchener (1850–1916)!

only catfish ever caught in the Serpentine.

The man's technique and attitude seemed to rub off on the boys, who concentrated harder when he was around and tried to emulate his calm, measured ways. They also noted how carefully he unhooked his fish and how gently he returned them.

Perhaps the oddest thing of all about the tall, thin fisherman was that throughout the 30 years he fished the Serpentine he noted down the length and weight of every single fish he caught – however tiny and apparently insignificant – in a series of expensive-looking leather-bound notebooks. Each page had a heading giving the date and some brief notes about the weather, then below came a single line for each fish. In all there were 60 notebooks, which must have contained the details of thousands of fish in his tiny, neat hand.

Why the thin fisherman did all this, no one knew. Some said he was a disappointed Oxford academic who had turned to fishing as a relief from the iniquities of academic life. Others said (bizarrely!) that he was probably a spy. No one ever found out. Then, on the first day of the season one year, he failed to turn up and was never heard of or seen again.

Mayfair Chapel
Marriage à la Mode

Opposite Crew House in Curzon Street stood, until the end of the 19th century, one of London's strangest churches. The Mayfair Chapel was, until the Marriage Act of 1754, a continual thorn in the side of the authorities because it was here that the eccentric clergyman the Reverend Alexander Keith conducted marriage ceremonies for anyone who turned up at any time of the day or night, with absolutely no questions asked.

For young runaways and the romantically inclined in an age when marriages were so often a matter of convenience, the Mayfair Chapel was a godsend, as it were. People in authority hated it because it represented a threat to the plans they had for their own offspring, but Alexander Keith knew the law: he was perfectly entitled to do what he was doing. And

BELOW: *The Serpentine in Hyde Park was the haunt of the thin fisherman who practised his sport here for decades, recording each and every one of his catches.*

ABOVE: *Despite their huge size, the Wellington Arch and the rampant horses have been moved several times in their history, yet no-one seems to be able to decide what to call the monuments.*

the chapel's popularity can be judged by the fact that in just one year – 1742 – he married no fewer than 700 couples, and all with neither licence nor banns.

Parliament launched several attempts to change the law to make these marriages illegal, but it immediately abandoned the attempt when its members – the Lords in particular – realized that to do so would be to make many of their own grandchildren illegitimate.

Among the most famous marriages conducted at the Mayfair Chapel was that between the Duke of Hamilton and Elizabeth Dunning, one of the great beauties of Georgian England. The couple were in such a hurry that an old brass washer had to be used in place of a gold ring!

Wellington Arch
Horsing Around

Everything about the Wellington Arch is eccentric. First, there's its name: according to official publications it is indeed called the Wellington Arch, but it lies at the top of Constitution Hill and is often referred to as the Constitution Arch; to add to the confusion, when it was moved here in 1883, it was known as the Green Park Arch.

Whatever we call it, the arch was never supposed to be where it is now. When it was first erected in 1828 it stood about 100 yards from its current position, right in front of the Duke of Wellington's (1769–1852) Apsley House – or No. 1 London, as it is usually known.

The arch originally supported a vast 40-ton statue of Wellington, but this was considered so ugly that it was quickly removed. When the main road was

ABOVE: *Ghosts seem to haunt Linley Sambourne House, whose rooms have remained unaltered for more than a century.*

widened in the 1880s, the whole arch was moved to its current position, and a new statue placed on top. Just like the arch, the new statue can't make up its mind what to be called: some refer to it as the Quadriga, after the carriage and four horse it depicts; to others it is the Peace Monument.

A delightfully eccentric anecdote relates to the sculpture: the artist who made it – the now largely forgotten Adrian Jones – was so pleased with his work that when it was completed he invited half a dozen of his friends to have dinner with him inside the body of one of the horses. As each of the horses is twice life-size, there was plenty of room; the friends ate four courses, and by all accounts passed a most enjoyable evening.

Linley Sambourne House
Punch *Preserved*

Great houses often survive with their interiors intact, but the interiors of more ordinary houses tend to vanish without trace. Linley Sambourne House is a glorious exception.

The house, named after the cartoonist who lived here from 1874 to 1910, embodies perfectly the tastes of a well-to-do though by no means aristocratic household of the mid-Victorian period. When Sambourne and his young wife moved here, they decorated the four-year-old house in the then fashionable style, characterized by heavy velvet drapes, William Morris wallpapers, ornate Turkish carpets, and a vast clutter of china ornaments.

Sambourne earned his living as a cartoonist, mostly for the magazine *Punch*, for almost half a century. Most of his drawings were completed in this house, and numerous examples of his work can be seen here, along with his photographs – like many artists of the time, he was fascinated by this still-new art form.

By sheer luck the house remained largely unchanged through the 20th century. The Sambournes' son Roy inherited the property and hardly touched it – probably because he never married. When he died he left the house to his elder sister Maud. She, too, was passionate about preserving it intact, largely because – as she said herself – she'd been so happy there as a child. Her daughter Anne then used the house until, at a party in 1957, Anne proposed that she and her friends, who included the Poet Laureate Sir John Betjeman (1906–84), should found a Victorian Society to preserve not only this house and its contents but also to work for the preservation of other similar examples of Victorian style – a style that had by now become hugely unpopular. Tours of the house can be made by arrangement today.

The Inadvertent Fisherman
Roach Attack

It is quite common in London to see geese or swans flying overhead. Along the Thames, right into the heart of the City, herons stalk the shallows, and various wildlife organizations inform us that owls roost in Parliament Square, while kestrels hover above the Commercial Road. In fact, anywhere in the vicinity of London's bigger parks can be relied on to produce the odd bit of wildlife: reports of ducks wandering across Kensington High Street with ducklings in tow are quite common. A local newspaper, however, once carried a report of a far more bizarre wildlife encounter in Kensington.

A gentleman was walking home from work one autumn evening. He'd got half way up Kensington Church Street when he received what he described to the newspaper reporter as 'a terrific blow to the side of the head'. In fact, the blow was so hard that it knocked the man out, and he had to be taken to hospital.

One of the witnesses who'd helped the injured man into a local house, where brandy was administered, described an extraordinary circumstance that appears to have accounted for the knock-out blow. When the witness ran to the aid of the hapless victim, he spotted a large fish lying on the pavement nearby. Being a fisherman, he knew that this was not the sort of fish that would have been bought at a fishmonger's: it was a roach, a common freshwater fish that is completely inedible. The witness told the newspaper that at first he could not understand how the fish came to be lying in the street, but as he helped the man out of his coat he noticed something very odd indeed. The injured man's head and the shoulder of his coat were dusted here and there with fish scales; the scales were without question from the dead roach that had been found at the scene.

When the newspaper compiled its report on the incident it quoted a professor of zoology as saying that the man was almost certainly felled by a roach dropped by a passing bird, possibly a heron or cormorant. Curiously – the paper noted with glee – the injured man was called Mr Chub!

Leighton House
Arabian Nights

From the outside, this large red-brick house looks little different from dozens of others in this prosperous suburb of west London, but Leighton House has one of the oddest interiors of any in the capital.

It was built for the painter Lord Leighton (1830–96) to his own designs and those of his great friend the architect George Aitchison. The house reveals – uniquely – the Victorian passion for exotic architecture. Much of the house is as Leighton left it, including the huge, beautifully lit studio and the Silk Room, with its numerous pictures by Leighton's contemporaries and friends. There are works by the pre-Raphaelite artists Edward Burne-Jones (1833–98) and John Everett Millais (1829–96), as well as George Frederic Watts (1817–1904).

The most extraordinary room in the house is the Arab Hall. Based on drawings made by Aitchison of

OPPOSITE: *Leighton House, particularly the Arab Hall, is a monument to one man's passion for exotic architecture.*

(64km), but at 10 miles it was one of the wonders of Edwardian England.

Hardly had the public got used to this remarkable long-distance underground railway, than the company who ran the trains introduced something even more remarkable. When London's first railway escalator began operating at Earl's Court Station, on the Piccadilly Line, in 1911, the passengers were too terrified to use it. The railway company was aghast – they'd paid huge sums to have the equipment fitted, but it would all be wasted if no one would dare use it. Then someone had a bright idea: why not employ someone to use the escalator throughout the day, to give the public confidence?

The idea was accepted, and 'Bumper' Harris, a man with a wooden leg, was thereafter employed for a number of years to go up and down the escalator all day long. Soon, the public began to realize that if a man with one leg could use this remarkable new transportation system safely, there was no reason why they too shouldn't be able to. Of course, Bumper (about whom almost nothing else is known) did his job too well: the public soon thought nothing of using the new moving staircase, and he was out of a job!

the banqueting room at the Moorish palace at La Zisa in Sicily, the Arab Hall is an extraordinarily beautiful room, specifically designed to make use of Lord Leighton's vast collection of 16th- and 17th-century tiles from Damascus, Cairo and Rhodes. The room includes a fountain, a cupola with stained glass, and alcoves filled with intricate latticework.

Bumper Harris
Escalator Man

When London's Piccadilly Line was completed in 1906 it was the longest underground train line in the city, covering more than 10 miles (16km). It was later extended to 32 miles (52km), and then finally over 40

Carlyle's House
Smoker's Peril

The Victorian writer Thomas Carlyle (1795–1881) lived in a Queen Anne house in Cheyne Row, Chelsea, from the time he came to London in 1834 until his death in 1881. He loved this cranky old house – which, remarkably, remains today exactly as he left it with his hat still on a peg in the hall, as well as his furniture, books and pictures; even his tin bath is still in situ.

Carlyle and his wife had a famously stormy relationship; one of their friends is reported to have said: 'Carlyle and Mrs Carlyle were made for each other. When they married, God intended that only two rather than four people should be unhappy.' She

ABOVE: *Marching in step is forbidden on Albert Bridge as a protective measure against the risk of the whole edifice tumbling into the River Thames.*

hated the smell of tobacco, and when Alfred, Lord Tennyson came to call the two men had to lean into the basement kitchen chimney to smoke in order to avoid a severe telling-off.

Though he is little read today, Carlyle was once considered a very great author; his *Sartor Resartus* was a bestseller, and in this old house he wrote many of the other books that made him famous in his lifetime, including *The French Revolution* and *Frederick the Great*. Many of the great literary figures of Victorian England were regular guests – among them Charles Dickens (1812–70), John Ruskin (1819–1900) and the poet and essayist Leigh Hunt (1784–1859), famously caricatured by Dickens as Mr Skimpole in *Bleak House*. The house is now owned by the National Trust and is open to the public.

Albert Bridge
The Rhythm Method

Albert Bridge might look like just another bridge over the Thames. But it is, in fact, highly unusual. It was built by R.M. Ordish in 1873, with three spans and what is known as a 'straight link' suspension system. Each half of the bridge is supported by wrought-iron bars attached to the top of two highly ornamented towers. Meanwhile, the side girders along the parapets are suspended, making the bridge a curious mix of cantilever and suspension.

What makes it even more unusual is that an original toll house still stands on the south side of the bridge, together with a sign – placed here when the bridge was first erected – which states that soldiers must not march in step across the bridge: the rhythm created could trigger movements that might damage it or even cause it to collapse altogether.

Crosby Hall
Moving House

It is a regular enough occurrence for people to move house. However, it is much less common for a house itself to move! Nevertheless, this is the curious history of Crosby Hall in Cheyne Walk, Chelsea. Crosby Hall originally stood in Bishopsgate in the City of London. Built by Sir John Crosby, a wealthy wool merchant, between 1466 and 1475, some 450 years later it was moved stone by stone to its present site after being threatened with demolition. The original roof and oriel window have survived, and the house is otherwise substantially unaltered, unique for being the last remaining example of a medieval London merchant's house.

Japanese Peace Pagoda
Calm in the City

Battersea Park, on the south bank of the Thames opposite fashionable Chelsea, is easily overlooked. It has a pretty lake and tree-lined walks and avenues, but since Victorian times and the disappearance of

ABOVE: *The Japanese Peace Pagoda, an impressive example of Japanese architecture, is in keeping with the slightly abstract and esoteric nature of Battersea Park.*

the Battersea Park Fun Fair in the mid-1970s, few Londoners bother to visit it – which is a pity because where the park runs alongside the river stands one of London's most exotic and beautiful monuments: the Japanese Peace Pagoda.

Completed in 1985 in Portland stone and fir wood, and built by Buddhist monks, the pagoda was intended as a peace offering to London. The design has much in common with both the Chinese and Indian traditions of Buddhist buildings, and it houses gilded statues of the Buddha in alcoves, each symbolizing a stage in the Buddha's development, from birth to nirvana, or enlightenment, and then death.

Crapper & Co.
Lavatorial

Right through the Middle Ages and well into the 17th century, one of London's biggest problems was the lack of public loos. At home, people simply used

RIGHT: *Although improbable-sounding, Mr Thomas Crapper really did invent the first really effective flushing loo. Crapper's factory was in Chelsea, where his company still has an office.*

a bucket or pot and then threw the contents into the gutter or the Thames. Many people simply relieved themselves in the open on the street, but the more delicately disposed and, of course, ladies, found this unacceptable. The solution was provided by 'human loos'. These were men and women who wore voluminous black capes and carried a bucket. When you needed the loo, you looked for the nearest man or woman with a cape and bucket and gave them a farthing. You then sat on the bucket while they stood above you, surrounding you with their cape. The perfect portable loo!

By the 19th century, the proud imperial nation, with its conviction that technology should be both attractive and functional, began to produce public loos that were veritable cathedrals, filled with ornate tiles and gleaming pipes and cisterns. Many of the loos themselves were made by Thomas Crapper (1836–1910), inventor of the modern flushing loo, who had a factory on the King's Road. His porcelain loos carried a tiny, beautifully executed logo of a bee (the Latin for 'bee' is *apis*– a piss!).

One glorious public loo stood on Holborn until the 1980s, when it was scheduled for demolition. So beautiful was it, though, that it was saved and transported to the Victoria and Albert Museum. Its cisterns are glass and used to host goldfish – to the delight of those needing to spend a penny.

Sloane Square Station
The Flying River

Sloane Square Underground Station is, superficially, nothing out of the ordinary. Built at the end of the 19th century on the District Line, it served the grand residents of Eaton Square and Belgravia. When the engineers got to work on it, however, they discovered there was a river running right through the site.

The River Westbourne rises to the north-west of Hyde Park (hence Westbourne Terrace and Westbourne Grove) and originally flowed through the park – enabling 18th-century engineers to build the Serpentine – and on towards Sloane Square and, ultimately, the Thames.

It was some time before the engineers came up with the solution that makes Sloane Square one of the oddest stations on the whole Underground network. The answer was to construct a huge pipe, more than 4 feet (1 metre) in diameter, to carry the river over the platforms and railway lines. To this day, if you find yourself at Sloane Square Station, look up and you can see the massive pipe still in position, with the River Westbourne coursing through it.

Fulham Bottle Kiln
Pottery Class

Despite its popularity with the wealthy, Fulham has little of historic interest to commend it other than the old Bishop's Palace on the banks of the Thames. But, hemmed in by modern office blocks and houses, there is one bizarre little remnant of the past in the New King's Road. This is the early 19th-century bottle kiln, the last vestige of a pottery that existed here from 1672 until well into the 20th century.

The pottery was started by John Dwight, a lawyer with an amateur interest in pottery who was one of the first to develop highly glazed, porcelain-like pots. His new wares were much sought after, and he was commissioned to make busts of the rich and famous

from the works he established in what was then an entirely rural area.

The business expanded, and Dwight was still here making pots until his death in 1703. His family continued with the business, despite increasing competition from Midlands potteries such as Wedgwood. When the last of the Dwights left the business in 1864, it was sold to the Bailey family, and then in 1890 to the Cheavins, who introduced the highly collectable white earthenware 'Fulham' vases. Most of the pottery's buildings were burned down during the First World War (1914–18) and the factory never reopened, but the beautifully constructed bottle kiln – the name derives from its shape (an upturned bottle) survives.

London Wetland Centre
On the Waterfront

Nothing quite like this exists anywhere else in the world – a wildlife reserve covering more than 105 acres close to the heart of one of the world's biggest cities. The mixture of habitats created from these disused waterworks – the reservoirs once supplied Londoners with clean water – include grassland, mudflats and reedbeds; there are more than 30 ponds and lakes, nearly three miles of walkways, 27,000 trees and more than 200,000 aquatic plants.

There are hides from which to observe the bird life, and visitors are presented with binoculars for the duration of their tour. Species you might be lucky enough to see, depending on the time of year, include grebe, cormorant, heron, kingfisher, tern, wigeon, mallard, coot and tufted duck. Children are given little nets and allowed to fish for larvae and water insects, which staff can then help them identify.

Manton's Guns
Stand and deliver

To this day the name Manton brings to mind some of the best guns ever made. Joe Manton, who lived at the end of the 18th century, made all kinds of guns:

LEFT: *Amid high-rise modern developments, the Fulham Bottle Kiln now stands disused, a ghostly reminder of a former local industry.*

shotguns of all bore sizes, from 4 (big enough to bring down an elephant) to 28 (as light as a walking stick), as well as pistols and rifles. Most of his pistols were bought for personal protection, as at the time there was only a rudimentary and often corrupt police force. Travellers were always particularly vulnerable. Indeed, it was said that on a journey from London to Norwich a man had at least a fifty-fifty chance of being attacked and robbed.

On one occasion, Manton himself had been travelling across Hounslow Heath on the outskirts of west London, along the main road towards Bath. The heath had for centuries been infamous for its highwaymen and thieves, but for those heading west there was no avoiding it. Manton was travelling on business, and as it was daylight he thought he had little to fear. Then the coach lurched to a halt and he heard the dreaded shout, 'Stand and deliver!' He stuck his head out of the carriage window and found himself staring down the barrel of one of his own guns. Arguing with a highwayman, even for an instant, usually proved fatal, but Manton was so outraged he could not keep silent.

'Why damn it, you rascal!' he reportedly bellowed. 'I'm Joe Manton and that's one of my pistols you've got. How dare you try to rob me!'

'Oh,' said the highwayman coolly, 'you're Joe Manton are you? Well you charged me 10 guineas for this pistol, which was a damned swindle, though I admit it's a damned good barker. Now I mean to be quits with you. Hand over 10 guineas and I'll let you go because you're Joe Manton, though I know you have at least £50 about you.'

Speechless with rage, Manton swallowed his pride and handed over the money, but he never forgave the highwayman for effectively getting one of his pistols for nothing. To ensure it never happened again, Manton made himself a special double gun with barrels nearly 2 feet (0.6 metres) long. He called it the Highwayman's Master, and carried it with him whenever he travelled. Many years later a highwayman again stopped him. This time Manton was travelling towards London and as good as his word he whipped out his special gun and shot the man dead. History, regrettably, does not record whether it was the same highwayman who'd taken his 10 guineas all those years before.

ABOVE: *Deepest fenland comes to town at the extraordinary London Wetland Centre in Barnes.*

BELOW: *Gunmaker Joseph Manton was furious when he was held up by a man using a gun of his own design and making.*

South & South-east London

Long neglected in favour of the more fashionable north, south London is a glorious region of vibrant street markets, Georgian terraces and once-grand Italianate villas. And hidden away among the apparently ordinary are wonderful oddball gems, such as the house once lived in by Catherine of Aragon, the windmill now left high and dry in the middle of multicultural Brixton, human blood sculptures and, of course, watch out for those dinosaurs!

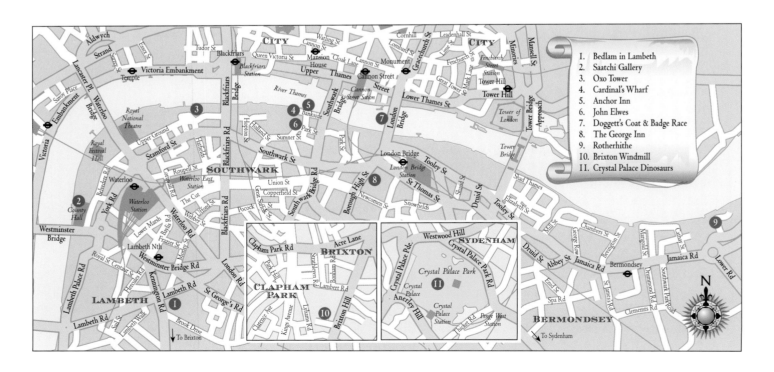

1. Bedlam in Lambeth
2. Saatchi Gallery
3. Oxo Tower
4. Cardinal's Wharf
5. Anchor Inn
6. John Elwes
7. Doggett's Coat & Badge Race
8. The George Inn
9. Rotherhithe
10. Brixton Windmill
11. Crystal Palace Dinosaurs

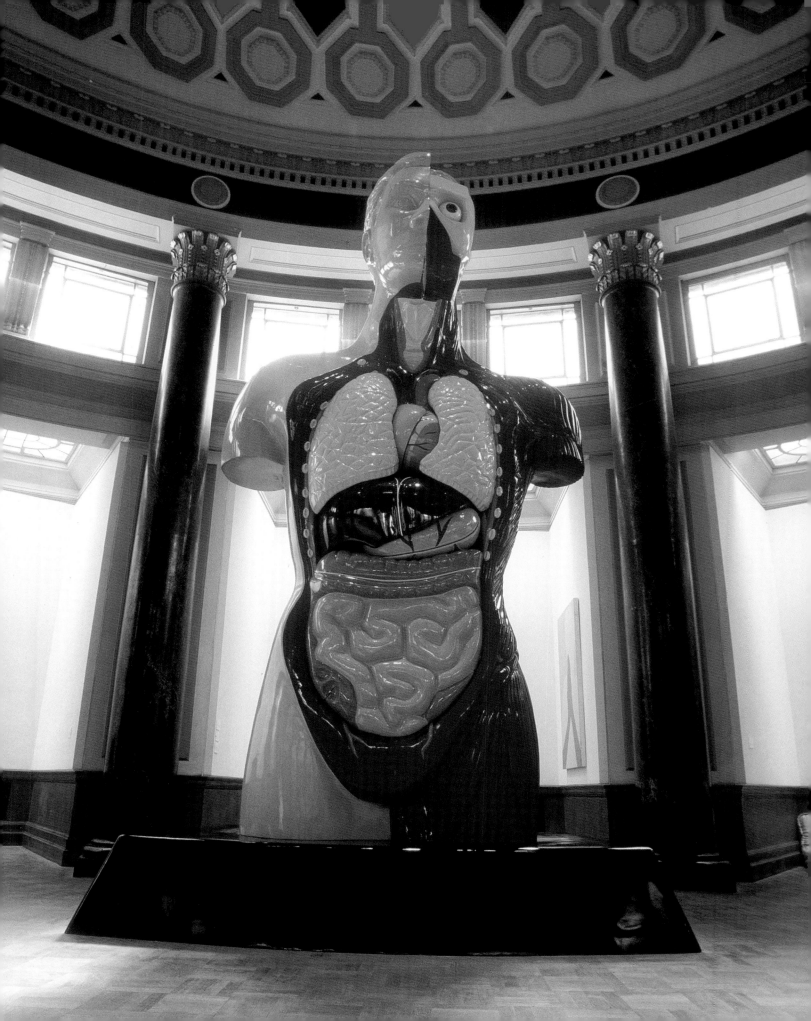

Pickled sheep, Victorian dinosaurs and a village in the town

Bedlam in Lambeth
'Guaranteed to Amuse'

Few people today realize that the splendidly grand building that now houses the Imperial War Museum just south of the river in Lambeth is the very place from which we get the word 'bedlam'.

The original Bethlehem Hospital was built just outside the City walls at Bishopsgate in 1250. It was then the priory of St Mary Bethlehem, with an ancient duty shared by all religious houses to give succour to the poor and needy. A little over a century later, records reveal that the priory had added on buildings specifically designed to house the mentally ill. Early attitudes to the mentally ill were, by modern standards, appalling: patients were shackled or kept permanently chained to the wall; they were never washed and were fed entirely on scraps of food; therapy consisted of ducking in freezing water or whipping. After the Dissolution of the Monasteries, the priory buildings became a hospital specifically required to take those who had 'entirely lost their wits and God's great gift of reasoning, the whiche only distinguisheth us from the beast.'

In 1676, the hospital moved again – this time to just outside Moorgate, to the north of the City. Designed by Robert Hooke, the beautiful classical building concealed a dreadful regime, with patients packed into insufficient space and no attempt at any kind of hygiene. By this time, London's wealthy and middle classes had begun to see Bethlehem Hospital as a sort of circus or amusement park. Every weekend hundreds of visitors arrived to be shown around: it was a

LEFT: *Among the most famous of all Hogarth's depictions of London life is his portrayal of the horror of Bedlam.*

PREVIOUS PAGE: *A giant version of an anatomical model of a child by Brit Pack darling Damien Hirst dominates one area of the Saatchi Gallery.*

trip 'guaranteed to amuse and lift the spirits', said one commentator.

Sadly, there is evidence that the warders deliberately worked the patients up before these visits to make them behave even more wildly than they would have otherwise. By now, the hospital was known as Bedlam and the word quickly became synonymous with any scene of chaos. Most of the hospital's income came from paying visitors, so it was important to put on a good show. It took another century – until the 1770s – before more enlightened hospital governors decided to stop all visits of this kind. Whips only stopped being used, however, in the early 19th century, when George III went mad and his plight aroused widespread sympathy.

By the early 1800s, plans had been drawn up for a new hospital on marshland south of the river. The domed building designed by James Lewis was finished in 1815, and the patients were brought across London from Moorfields in a long line of Hackney cabs. And here they stayed until 1930, when a new hospital was built at Addington in Surrey. In 1936, after much dithering about the fate of the old buildings, it was decided that they would provide an excellent home for the Imperial War Museum.

ABOVE: *Damien Hirst made a name for himself by preserving animals in formaldehyde in the name of Art. His work makes up just a part of the bizarrely wonderful Saatchi Gallery.*

Saatchi Gallery
From Cows to Car Oil

County Hall, on the south bank of the River Thames, almost opposite the Houses of Parliament, is a massive, decidedly pedestrian-looking building. Started in 1909, but astonishingly not completed until 1963, this was the hub of London governance until Prime Minister Margaret Thatcher (b.1925) abolished the Greater London Council in the 1980s.

On the ground floor, many of the original timber-panelled rooms survive in an unmodernized state. But now these staid Edwardian office rooms, where it is easy to imagine clerks in wing collars perched on their high stools, are home to one of the world's most bizarre art collections.

Charles Saatchi (b.1943), the former advertising mogul and notorious devotee of the so-called Brit Pack generation of contemporary artists, moved his collection here in 2003, and the old rooms are now

home to such weird installations as Damien Hirst's cow cut in half and preserved in formaldehyde; sculptures made from human blood and used car oil; cows' heads covered in live maggots; and giant ashtrays filled with thousands of real cigarette butts... you get the picture!

Oxo Tower
Something to Beef About

In the early part of the 20th century, London was still a rather strait-laced place: advertising was considered rather vulgar – to the extent that it was banned on the sides of buildings. In part, this attitude represented an attempt to tidy up after the chaos of earlier centuries, when shopkeepers and tradesmen had put signs outside their shops and then tried to outdo each other by gradually making their signs bigger or attaching them to long poles, until narrow streets would be dark all day because of the shadows cast by the countless signs.

The first buses were also covered in adverts and then posters began to creep up the sides of buildings – until the authorities called a halt. Tall edifices, as these began to appear, would have provided excellent sites for advertisements and the authorities were horrified at the prospect. One or two advertisers, though, were determined to get round the ban, and in at least one strange instance they got away with it.

On the south bank of the Thames, near Blackfriars Bridge, a tower was built above a warehouse. The tower survives, and is now home to a very fashionable restaurant which offers diners a magnificent view along the river from their tables. At the top of the tower and visible from miles away there is an advertisement for the famous Oxo beef cube. The advert has been here since the building was first erected and it escaped the ban on advertising on buildings by incorporating the advertisement – the letters 'OXO' – into the building's very structure: the three giant letters are, in fact, three vast windows filled with red glass.

LEFT: *The immediately recognizable Oxo Tower on the South Bank cleverly uses windows to form letters, all in an effort to get round an advertising ban.*

Cardinal's Wharf
If the Cap Fits...

This is a tall, narrow house, once part of a terrace, that overlooks the Thames on the south bank of the river opposite St Paul's Cathedral. It is a most bizarre survivor – the earliest and last-remaining of the many Bankside houses that once lined the river here where Shakespeare's plays were first performed.

The house is still privately owned, and has an illustrious history: when Henry VIII's wife Catherine of Aragon (1485–1536) arrived from Spain she stayed here, and two centuries later when Christopher Wren was building St Paul's he too stayed in the house to supervise the work on his great cathedral.

Although it has been altered over the years, the house is, nevertheless, basically 16th- century. It stands almost next door to the recreated Globe Theatre, and running down one side – sadly now closed to the public – is one of London's narrowest thoroughfares, Cardinal Cap Alley.

Anchor Inn
Thames-side Crank

One of the few really old buildings along the Thames at Bankside, the Anchor is largely 18th-century. Until the 1970s it was still one of those now-vanished pubs that attracted a few elderly locals who spent their evenings in the tiny bar. Since then, of course, the whole building has been opened up, antique bits and pieces have been hung from the walls, food is served and the pub is very much on the tourist circuit. But, that said, the pub has not been over-restored or over-commercialized. It still looks and feels like a cranky old riverside pub, 18th-century in character and therefore very rare along a riverside so massively redeveloped since the war. The odd cupboards hidden here and there are said to have been used to hide escapees from the nearby Clink Prison (though there is no real evidence for this). Parts of the building may well date back to Shakespeare's time, when it was known as the Castle on the Hoop; there was certainly a pub here in the 15th century, when this part of Southwark was a mass of brothels.

ABOVE: *An ornate plaque on Cardinal's Wharf records some of the colourful history of one of London's oldest private houses.*

BELOW: *The Anchor Inn is filled with odd cupboards and hidey-holes in which escaped prisoners from the nearby Clink Prison are said to have hidden.*

John Elwes
The Southwark Miser

John Elwes was born *c.* 1730 into a family of notorious misers. They had lived in Southwark for generations, and made their money from brewing. His

mother is said to have died from malnutrition in spite of having tens of thousands of pounds in the bank, and although John was apparently an exceptionally bright child, he rarely opened a book after leaving school; in fact, as the desire to make money grew he gave up everything else – including riding, which had been a passion in his youth.

In his twenties John began to visit his uncle, Sir Harvey Elwes, but he always changed into rags before he reached the house, so terrified was he that his uncle, an infamous miser, would be offended at his decent clothes and disinherit him. Uncle and nephew would sit by a fire made with one stick and completely in the dark, sharing a glass of wine until bedtime; they would then creep upstairs, still in the dark, to save the cost of a candle.

Later, when John Elwes himself was bitten by the miser's bug, he refused to educate his own sons because he thought it would give them grand ideas about spending money rather than keeping it. When he came into his inheritance, Elwes became fanatically stingy. He would walk from one end of London to the other in the heaviest rain rather than part with sixpence for a coach; he ate maggot-infested meat; he would never light a fire to dry his clothes; he wore a wig that had reputedly been thrown into a ditch by a beggar, and a coat that had gone green with age – it had belonged to a long-dead ancestor and had been found blocking a hole in the wall of the house. On the occasions that he rode out of London instead of walking, he would carry an egg or two in his pocket for food and sleep in a hedge rather than pay the cost of lodgings; and he always rode his horse on the grass verge instead of on the road for fear that his horse's shoes would wear out too quickly. He owned houses all over London as well as an estate in Suffolk, but took a few pieces of furniture with him each time he

ABOVE: *Southwark Cathedral was the last resting place of one of London's most eccentric misers.*

travelled about rather than furnish each house.

Yet, in spite of his parsimony, John Elwes rarely collected a gambling debt if it was owed to him by someone he liked, and he was himself a very keen gambler, parting with thousands at a go when the mood took him. He could also be generous and considerate: he once rode 60 miles (100km) to help two elderly spinsters threatened by an ecclesiastical court, and he served as a Member of Parliament for 10 years. He died in 1789 and was buried in the graveyard of Southwark Cathedral. He left over £750,000 to his two sons.

Doggett's Coat and Badge Race
Oldest and oddest

The Guild of Watermen was once one of the most powerful guilds in London. From medieval times, watermen were vital for transporting goods and people up and down the river, particularly in winter, when the roads – even between the City and Westminster – were often impassable. They also helped unload ships in the Port of London, collected bodies and other refuse from the river, and operated the fixed ferries. Until well into the 19th century, they opposed the building of new bridges on the grounds that these would lessen their trade. Today, of course, the watermen have largely vanished, but their long centuries on the river are commemorated in the oldest – and oddest – continually run sporting event in Britain, Doggett's Coat and Badge Race.

The race, which takes place in July each year, was the brainchild of actor and manager of the Drury Lane Theatre, Thomas Doggett. When he died in 1721, Doggett left money so that a race could be held in his honour every year in perpetuity. Originally the watermen used their heavy wooden rowing boats, but the 4½-mile (7-km) course from London Bridge to Chelsea is now completed in light fibreglass skiffs, and since 1950 amateur rowers as well as professional watermen have been allowed to compete.

The rowers compete for a bizarre array of prizes. These were laid out in Doggett's original, will which left money for 'procuring yearly on the first day of August and forever thereafter the following: five pounds for a badge of silver weighing 12oz and representing Liberty, to be given to be rowed by six young watermen… eighteen shillings for cloathe for a livery, whereon the said badge is to be put, one pound one shilling for making up on the said livery and buttons and appurtenances to it and thirty shillings to the clerk of the Watermen's Hall all which I would have to be continued yearly in commemoration of his majesty King George's happy accession to the British throne.'

ABOVE: *Doggett's Coat and Badge Race commemorates the life of actor Thomas Doggett, who died in 1721.*

throughout the long centuries when all transport was by horse.

In former times, there were at least half a dozen galleried inns in London. They were built round a courtyard, and the rooms on each level gave onto a walkway or gallery. The courtyard enabled coaches to enter and be unloaded in the midst of the inn space. On the ground floor would have been the public rooms for drinking and eating, and above, entered via the external galleries, would have been the bedrooms. The George retains this arrangement, and though you can no longer stay at the inn you may still drink in the bars below.

The oldest of The George's bars still has its 18th-century interiors – with tavern clock, crooked timber floors, two fireplaces and benches built into the walls. Sadly this small 'tap room', as it is known, is no longer used as a bar but it can still be visited.

Only one side of what was originally a four-sided inn still exists, but when you look up from the

The George Inn
Playing to the Gallery

The George Inn deserves to be much better known, because it is London's last representative of a style of building that was common

RIGHT: *The George Inn is a most extraordinary survivor, looking today much as it would have done in Shakespeare's day.*

ABOVE: *These beautifully carved life-size figures of children are located on Peter Hills School in Rotherhithe and date back to the early 18th century.*

courtyard you can at least be sure that this is an authentic glimpse into London's past – a past that Charles Dickens and William Shakespeare would have recognized; Dickens even mentions The George by name in *Little Dorrit*.

There has been an inn on this site since the 14th century, though the present building dates from just after a huge fire which destroyed most of Southwark in 1676. Throughout the 18th century and earlier, The George was the starting point for thousands of giant wagons leaving London each week for Sussex, Kent and Surrey. Stage coaches carrying passengers ran almost continually day and night, and the inn would have been a frantic scene of constant activity. The arrival of the railways put paid to coaching inns, but The George survived into the 20th century by using its yard as a hop market. It was nearly demolished in the 1930s by the railway company that owned it at that time, but at the last minute the company decided instead to give what remained of the building to the National Trust.

Rotherhithe
A Village in the Town

Rotherhithe is a remarkably complete 18th-century village just a couple of miles downstream of London's Tower Bridge on the south side of the river. Strictly speaking, Rotherhithe is one long, winding street that follows the Thames from the old village centre almost as far as Deptford, a distance of 2 miles (3km). But today, the heart of the village – or at least the historic part – is centred round the church of St Mary.

By the middle of the 19th century, Rotherhithe – or Redriffe, as the diarist and naval administrator Samuel Pepys (1633–1703) called it – had descended from being a place of clean air and elegant houses where merchants lived to being one of the worst slums in London. Dickens described the houses here as 'so filthy and so confined that the very air would seem to be tainted… here is every imaginable sign of desolation and neglect… tottering houses, windows broken and patched… stagnant water everywhere.'

London's first enclosed wet dock was built here in 1699. Then, as the Surrey Docks developed in the 19th century, thousands of small, wretchedly built

ABOVE: *The Mayflower Inn, from which pilgrims left for America and the New World, lies at the heart of the village of Rotherhithe.*

workers' cottages were put up. Throughout this building period the old village survived, as indeed it survived the later wholesale demolition of many of those same little houses in the 1950s and 1960s.

Old Rotherhithe still has its dank, dripping lanes that wander down to the river. When you stand here you can understand why Jonathan Swift chose this seafarers' village as the birthplace for his fictional voyager, Lemuel Gulliver. Momentous journeys that changed the real world began here, too: it was from Rotherhithe that the *Mayflower* almost certainly began her history-changing voyage to America.

Today, the old village still retains a number of elegant 18th-century houses and 19th-century warehouses, now mostly restored. But central to historic Rotherhithe is the church, a beautiful yellow-and-red-brick building put up in 1714 by an unknown architect. Most of London's churches – including famous ones by Christopher Wren – had to be rebuilt or very substantially repaired after the Second World War, but St Mary's Rotherhithe is one of a small

number that completely escaped the ravages of bomb damage, fire or rebuilding. The spire was altered in the 19th century, but inside, the church is substantially as it was when this was a quiet village with only fields and marshland between it and London upriver.

St Mary's has most of its 18th-century woodwork, including panelling, communion rails and staircase, and there is an interesting monument to one Joseph Wade, whose job title was 'King's Carver at his Majesty's Shipyards at Deptford and Woolwich.' The church stands amid old trees, and if you leave the churchyard by the south gate you are faced with a lovely narrow, three-storey house built between 1690 and 1700. The Peter Hills School was established here in 1797, and two beautifully carved life-size figures of children stand in niches above the house door as a reminder of that time. The children may previously have adorned another building, as they were probably carved in about 1700. A little further along the winding street, to the west of the school, is an engine house built in 1821 as part of the works for Marc Brunel's magnificent Rotherhithe Tunnel under the river – an astonishing engineering feat for the time – which was completed between 1825 and 1843.

ABOVE: *Brixton Windmill was still grinding corn in the 1950s. However, it now stands almost forgotten in one of London's most vibrant districts.*

London, that sense of villages gathered together largely vanishes and it is difficult to believe that you are in what was once countryside. Brixton is in many ways the epitome of an inner-city urban area, yet tucked away down a side street is a bizarre relic of Brixton's rural past – a full-size Georgian windmill.

Brixton's windmill was built in 1816, when this area was still open countryside. In fact, this remained a landscape largely of fields and farms until the 1850s when plots began to be sold to speculative builders. By the 1860s, all the land round the windmill had been covered over with houses, and it seemed pointless to bring corn into the town when it could far more easily be ground by mills nearer to hand.

Yet remarkably, while every other windmill in London was quickly demolished, Brixton survived. At the beginning of the 20th century it was converted to run on gas, and it continued to mill corn until the 1950s when the local council took it over, restored it and then failed utterly to prevent vandals from wrecking it. The council still fails to look after properly one of the most interesting buildings in its care, despite its Grade 2 listing, and local youngsters continue to knock it about, but it is still worth a visit (by prior arrangement with the council).

Brixton Windmill
A Georgian Survivor

Many areas of London retain an almost ghostly sense of their past as villages. Kew is one example, with its village green surrounded by 18th-century houses, and Pinner, with its few crooked timber-framed buildings, is another. But when you get closer to the centre of

Crystal Palace Dinosaurs
Outrageous Monsters

One of London's strangest outdoor features is the Dinosaur Park at Crystal Palace. The life-size cast-concrete dinosaurs were placed in the park in 1854, several years before Charles Darwin published his theory of evolution, and they caused outrage at the time: they were clearly intended to demonstrate that life had not begun 4,000 years earlier as the Bible stated but revealed millions of years of evolutionary history.

The Dinosaur Park was built under the supervision of legendary architect Sir Joseph Paxton – the man who built the Crystal Palace. Paxton collaborated with Richard Owen, the Victorian scientist who had coined the term 'dinosaur', which means 'terrible lizard'. By the 1980s the park was in a sorry state, but the local council has since restored these remarkably

life-like creatures, repainted them and added a limestone cliff of the sort that would have been around when the dinosaurs ruled the earth. Among the creatures recreated are a giant ground sloth, a whole herd of Anoplotheria and a huge megalosaur, but the restorers decided not to add more recent dinosaur discoveries. The park is therefore an excellent record of our knowledge of dinosaurs as it was in the 1850s.

BELOW: *The life-size dinosaurs in Crystal Palace are a surprising and fairly frightening find for anyone on a quiet Sunday afternoon stroll.*

East London

Rough, tough and full of character, the East End was once a fearsome place that even the police avoided if they could. But as the river served to welcome trade from all parts of the world, the East End grew over the centuries and developed a culture of extraordinary richness and diversity. Inevitably, too, it has its wacky stories to tell – such as the train that was pulled by rope, the pub with a legendary ancient tunnel to the Tower of London, and the Moorish palace that is actually a sewage pumping station.

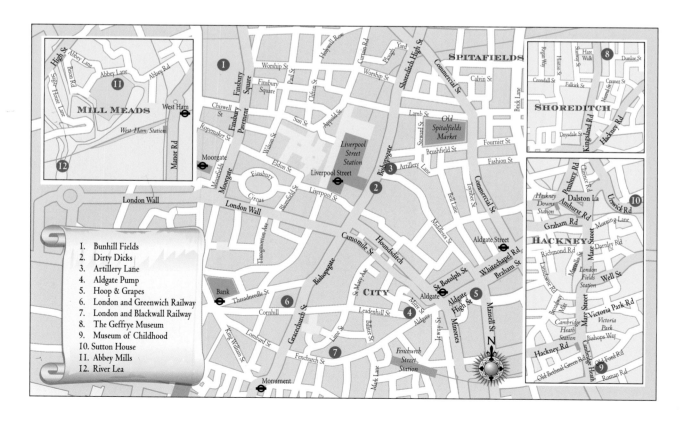

1. Bunhill Fields
2. Dirty Dicks
3. Artillery Lane
4. Aldgate Pump
5. Hoop & Grapes
6. London and Greenwich Railway
7. London and Blackwall Railway
8. The Geffrye Museum
9. Museum of Childhood
10. Sutton House
11. Abbey Mills
12. River Lea

Peculiar pubs aplenty and a museum that moves

Bunhill Fields
Dissenters' Graveyard

Lying behind modern offices in one of the busiest parts of central London is a small graveyard that seems to have no connection with its surroundings. This is Bunhill Fields, one of those ancient burial grounds that were once common just outside the City gates. It was a nonconformist burial ground for those religious dissenters who refused to accept the teaching of the Church of England.

Just north of the old Moorgate, Bunhill was once part of Finsbury Manor, and it was here in medieval times that the London apprentices came to practice archery on Sundays. There were three big fields here, but the name Bunhill is a mystery: it may be derived from 'Bone Hill', yet the name predates the graveyard by several centuries.

Bunhill has seen some grisly sights in its day: in the 1540s, huge carts came here day after day from St Paul's, removing centuries of human bones from the ancient charnel-house attached to the cathedral. A century later, the ground was enclosed by a wall and gates. It was designated as a burial ground for victims of the plague that raged in London in 1665, though there is no evidence that plague victims were brought here in any numbers.

By the mid-19th century, Bunhill Fields was typical of so many old London graveyards: bodies were piled on top of one another in graves until there was perhaps just a few inches of soil on the topmost corpse. This practice was blamed for the frequent outbreaks of cholera that affected Londoners, and so in 1852 the Burials Act closed the graveyards down.

Many similar burial grounds were subsequently built over, but here amid the offices and warehouses Bunhill has survived, though reduced in size. It boasts monuments to Susannah Wesley (mother of the famous Methodist preachers John and Charles), Daniel Defoe (*c.* 1660–1731), William Blake (1757–1827), and – the best-known non conformist of all, a man who spent many years in prison for his beliefs – John Bunyan (1628–88), author of *The Pilgrim's Progress*.

ABOVE: *Dirty Dicks was once owned by a broken-hearted eccentric who rarely washed and let the place go to rack and ruin, strangely making a fortune in the process.*

OPPOSITE AND PREVIOUS PAGE: *The bone-riddled ground of Bunhill Fields is the last resting place of those Londoners who refused to conform to the Church of England's rules on worship.*

Dirty Dicks
Rags to Riches

Many London pubs are far older than they might at first appear. In Bishopsgate, Dirty Dicks dates back to the early 18th century, even though the pub looks typically mid-Victorian. It was here that one of London's most extraordinary and eccentric characters once lived.

The story varies in its details, but it seems that Nathaniel Bentley, a local businessman and dandy who ran the pub, decided to get married. Everything was prepared, and the pub's dining rooms were laid out with beautiful flowers, cutlery, linen and a huge cake, but on the night before the wedding tragedy struck: the bride died. Distraught, Bentley sealed up the room and never opened it again. He also stopped washing, and only changed his clothes when they rotted and fell off him. 'What is the point of washing my hands, or anything else for that matter, when they will only be dirty again tomorrow?' he asked despondently. He allowed his pub to become one of the filthiest ale-houses in London, yet people flocked to it to see if it really was as bad as they'd been told. As a result Bentley made a fortune – a fortune he never spent because he bought nothing. He lived for nearly 40 years after being left in the lurch, finally dying in 1809.

The remnants of the old clothes that had been hung from the ceiling were only cleared out in the 1980s (they fell foul of new health and safety rules), but the pub still has a few fake rags here and there to remind us of its decidedly wacky past.

Artillery Lane
Minding the Shop

Before the bombs of the Second World War fell on London, large numbers of very early, even medieval, houses still stood in the city. Many survived the bombs, but the Corporation of London finished off most of the rest by giving the go-ahead to almost every request for demolition put before them in the 1960s. Yet by something little short of a miracle, some fascinating and even bizarre buildings survived the planning onslaught. One such is an extraordinary shop in Artillery Lane in Spitalfields.

The lane was first built in the late 1600s after centuries of use as a training ground by the artillery

company (hence the name), but the land had always been owned by one of the great religious houses – St Mary Spital – that were once common here in medieval times. Most of the original houses have long gone, but No. 56 remains, complete with its beautifully crafted shopfront, with a bowed window and ornate wooden carving. This rare gem is thought to date from between 1740 and 1750, and affords us an intriguing glimpse into what much of 18th-century London must once have been like.

Aldgate Pump
Drink Deep

There has been a pump here at the junction of Leadenhall Street and Fenchurch Street since at least the 13th century. It's been moved back and forth a few feet over the intervening years, but still stands only a few feet from its original spot. It was almost destroyed by the City authorities in the 1890s, but the protests of local people – surprisingly strong, given that the Victorians were not normally so sentimental about the past – saved it in the nick of time.

The pump we see today – made from stone, with a brass dog's-head ornament – was built in the early 1870s, but the original – which was set against the old Roman and later medieval gate (hence 'Ald gate') is marked on 16th- and 17th-century maps; it is also mentioned in John Stow's great survey of London (1598).

The pump was originally erected to tap into a spring that bubbled up here, called St Michael's Well. Suspicions were roused about the quality of the water

OPPOSITE ABOVE: *In Artillery Lane, this beautiful 18th-century shopfront has survived the ravages of time.*

OPPOSITE BELOW: *There has been a pump in the same spot in Aldgate since the 13th century.*

RIGHT: *The Hoop and Grapes is the City's oldest licensed premises, and even has a secret tunnel to the Tower of London.*

in the 1870s, so from then on water was piped to the pump from further afield. It continued in use until well into the 20th century, but once clean water was supplied universally to households, it became redundant.

Hoop & Grapes
Listening In

This is one of those strange old pubs that one would expect to have vanished from London decades ago. Records suggest that it is the oldest licensed premises in the City. Certainly its foundations, well beneath the modern road level, date from the 12th or 13th century, and the rest of the building is clearly ancient, leaning in that way that timber-framed buildings tend to with age. Experts tell us, though, that the building dates back to just after the Great Fire of 1666.

What makes the pub unique is that is still has a listening tube that runs from the cellar to the bars. This was installed so that the landlord could listen for seditious or malicious gossip – which, presumably, was more likely to occur while he was out of sight in the cellar.

There is good evidence that somewhere in the cellars there is a blocked entrance to a tunnel that runs from the pub to the nearby Tower of London. No doubt excavations at some time in the future will reveal whether there is any truth in this story.

London and Greenwich Railway
Ship on the Rails

The huge success of the earliest railways in the north of England meant that the rail network quickly spread, and before long the 'iron roadway' came to London. The earliest London service ran from the City to Greenwich. Crowds gathered in the 1830s and '40s to gaze at the extraordinary breathing monster that could pull huge loads without the assistance of horses. The new mode of transport was very popular with the travelling public – or at least with that sector of it wealthy enough to indulge in what was quite a luxury. But much as people admired the technology of steam, there were many complaints about the aesthetics of the whole enterprise.

ABOVE: *The London and Blackwall Railway must be one of the oddest railway companies ever created, as its trains were powered by rope pulleys.*

Chief among these was that somehow the engines were rather ugly. Letters were written in great quantities to the railway companies asking if they could not brighten up their dismal-looking locomotives. Of course, the first generation to experience steam engines judged them against the brightly coloured mail coaches that still dominated the national transportation system.

According to the then editor of the *Railway News*, the London and Greenwich Railway (L&GR) company took the complaints about the appearance of their engines very seriously. They studied the problem and after some time came up with a solution. Because the brick-built viaducts that carried the line into London looked rather like Roman aqueducts, a bright spark at the L&GR suggested to Braithwaite and Milner, who made the company's engines, that they build a locomotive in the style of a Roman galley.

A year later, huge crowds gathered at Cornhill, in the City, to watch the arrival of a train pulled by a very passable imitation of an ancient ship. Thereafter, much of the route was regularly lined with spectators eager to see this extraordinary engine, which was – as

its inventor had suggested – particularly impressive when viewed from the ground as it passed sedately over the company's viaducts. The only thing that spoiled the effect was the noise and the clouds of dense smoke.

Despite its initial popularity, though, the idea that locomotives should imitate ships did not catch on, and the London and Greenwich soon reverted to more practical-looking engines.

London and Blackwall Railway
Dragged to Blackwall

When the very first passengers boarded a train on the London and Blackwall Railway in 1836 (then known as the Commercial Railway), they were about to travel on what was one of the most bizarre railways ever built.

The railway was worked not by steam engines pulling carriages along the track, but by stationary engines fixed at either end of the route. A rope was attached to the fixed engines and this was used to drag the carriages along the rail. There was one rope for the up traffic and another for the down, each having a total length of about 8 miles (13km) and weighing 40 tons. And it was on this line that one of the earliest electric telegraph systems was used to tell the engineer at Blackwall or Fenchurch Street when to begin winding up or letting go his rope.

On that first journey, the down train, as it left Fenchurch Street, consisted of seven carriages. The two carriages at the front went through to Blackwall, the next carriage only as far as Poplar, and so on to the seventh carriage, which was left behind at Shadwell – the first station after Fenchurch Street. As the train approached Shadwell, the guard, who had to stand on a rickety platform in front of the carriage, pulled out a pin from the coupling just in time to allow the momentum of the carriage to carry it to its stopping point. The same process was repeated at each subsequent station, until finally the two remaining carriages ran up the terminal incline, and were brought to a stand at Blackwall Station. On the return journey, the carriage at each station was attached to the rope at a fixed hour, and then the whole series was set in motion simultaneously so that each carriage arrived at Fenchurch Street at appropriate intervals.

There were perpetual delays on the line owing to the rope breaking, and the cost of repairs and renewals was huge – so much so that within a few years of its inauguration the system was abandoned. However, it is a reminder that in the early days of the Industrial Revolution, the idea of railway transport threw up some decidedly eccentric innovations.

The Geffrye Museum
The Past Recreated

With its jaded air of former commercial prosperity, Kingsland Road, which runs from the City to Hackney, now seems an unlikely setting for a row of exquisite 18th-century almshouses. The Geffrye almshouses, which were built by Sir Robert Geffrye for the Ironmongers'

ABOVE: *Tucked away in an unlikely corner of the East End, the Geffrye Museum recreates interiors from a variety of historical periods.*

Company in 1715, now house one of the oddest yet most interesting exhibitions in the country.

Here, well away from the main tourist areas of London, you will find a remarkable collection of English furniture, pictures and other fittings in a series of chronologically arranged period rooms, dating from the early 17th century through to the 1960s and beyond. There is the dark, beautiful, early oak furniture and panelling of the Elizabethans, the light and elegance of a Georgian sitting room, a heavy Victorian interior, and a 1950s room filled with utility furniture and an early television. The best thing about the museum is that the interiors reflect in many instances the life of the less well-off, and the attention to detail is remarkable. Entry is free.

Museum of Childhood
Any Old Iron

The Bethnal Green Museum of Childhood would be fascinating enough just for its collection of toys, games, dolls' houses, model theatres, puppets, board games and books from almost every period, but it is also one of London's oddest buildings in that it has moved – quite literally – across the city.

The interior iron structure was originally part of the Victorian and Albert Museum in South Kensington, but it was moved to the East End in 1872 rather than be scrapped. Having been re-erected it was completely encased in brick by the architect James Wild, though the iron structure can still be seen. The outside was decorated by students from the National Art Training School (which in 1896 became the Royal College of Art), with murals depicting the arts, sciences and agriculture from designs by F.W. Moody, and the marble mosaic floor was put together by women prisoners from Woking Gaol.

BELOW: *The Museum of Childhood's iron superstructure started life in South Kensington and somehow ended up in Bethnal Green.*

Sutton House
Tudor Psychedelic

ABOVE: *A bizarre mix of Tudor panelling, ancient interiors and 1960s graffiti make Sutton House utterly unique.*

One of the oddest houses owned by The National Trust, Sutton House is a Tudor mansion left high and dry in one of the most run-down parts of Hackney. Despite its strange location amid housing estates and shopping centres, Sutton House is a real gem. Many of the rooms still have their Tudor panelling, early wall paintings and superb original fireplaces, though there are artefacts and decorative schemes that reflect far more recent owners.

Sutton House was built by Sir Ralph Sadleir, one of Henry VIII's courtiers, in 1535, on the edge of what was then the tiny village of Hackney. It would

have dazzled the locals when it was completed, because it was built in brick – which at that time was hugely expensive. The house passed through the hands of a series of wealthy merchants before becoming a girls' school in Victorian times. Gradually the city engulfed it – without, remarkably, damaging it significantly. But over time it declined as successive owners allowed it to decay; by the 1960s it had become a hippy squat, and the psychedelic murals painted in some of the rooms are still there, adding to the curious feel of the house, with its varied history.

Abbey Mills Pumping Station
Sewage Palace

This dotty-looking building, with its Moorish domes and towers resembling something from Asia or the Middle East, was, in fact, built in Victorian times (during a period of enthusiasm for all things Islamic) to disguise, of all things, a sewage works! The interior is even more bizarre, as it looks exactly like an Eastern Orthodox Church. The architect of this extraordinary confection was the man who built the Embankment along the Thames, Joseph Bazalgette (1819–91)

Bazalgette built the Embankment not so much to prettify the Thames or to create an easy route for traffic through London, but to provide somewhere to hide the massive sewers that were designed to take London's effluvia further downstream. The Embankment sewer scheme had been proposed after Parliament found it increasingly difficult to meet at all in summer because of the stink from the river. The Embankment was only part of the answer, and

ABOVE: *It may look like a splendid palace, but the Abbey Mills Pumping Station is just a typically ornate example of the Victorians' attempt to deal with London's sewage problem.*

Bazalgette was given responsibility for sorting out the whole of London's main drainage system – of which Abbey Mills became a part.

Like so many pumping stations, it had to be made to look like anything other than a sewage pumping station so as not to offend Victorian sensibilities. With a Moorish palace in their midst, Victorians could make-believe that the place had nothing whatsoever to do with distasteful bodily functions.

River Lea
Records in a London Sewer

The purer the water, the better the fishing. In general there is no arguing with that statement, but there are exceptions, and one or two of them are quite unbelievable.

The old River Lea that runs from Hertfordshire

down into North London, and from there joins the Thames in the East End, was once one of the cleanest rivers in the country. It was here that the great Izaak Walton (1593–1683) fished, and many of the experiences described in *The Compleat Angler* took place on this once glorious waterway. But as the City expanded and industry flourished, much of the river became too dirty to support anything worth fishing for. By the early decades of the 20th century, the River Lea was little more than an open sewer.

Then rumours began to spread that fish had been seen in one or two places in the London reaches of the river. This was remarkable enough, but local fishermen shook their heads in disbelief when it was also reported that the fish were in greatest numbers precisely at those place where sewer outfalls entered the river.

In Tottenham, a journalist from a fishing magazine went along to see what all the fuss was about. He found a gin-clear, fast-flowing stream that ran between high solid concrete banks. But it wasn't a stream at all – it was the sewage outfall. Nevertheless, the water running through it looked cleaner than the water in Hampshire's famous River Test, one of the best fishing rivers in England. Great shoals of fish were visible in the water, difficult to catch but far bigger than in most rivers.

In the two years that followed the discovery of the sewage-outfall fishery, the British records for gudgeon, bleak and dace were all broken by fish taken here. When scientists investigated, they discovered that the effluent was being so efficiently cleaned up that it was actually providing the fish with a protein-rich diet – hence their enormous average size.

BELOW: *The River Lea was once as dirty as an open sewer, but soon the sewage itself became so clean that it provided a nutritious diet for hungry fish.*

North London

As London spread north during the vast period of Victorian expansion it swallowed many ancient villages and hamlets – swallowed but didn't always destroy, which is why the quirky landmarks and the strange traditions of centuries still survive if you know where to look in and around what were once small communities on the high slopes. Thus in Highgate you can still swear on the horns and in Islington you can walk along a river that is not a river at all.

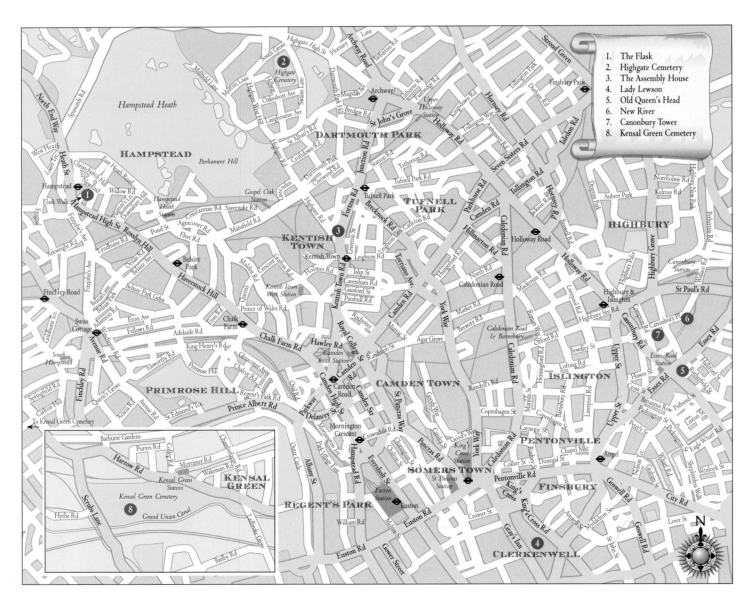

1. The Flask
2. Highgate Cemetery
3. The Assembly House
4. Lady Lewson
5. Old Queen's Head
6. New River
7. Canonbury Tower
8. Kensal Green Cemetery

A river that isn't a river, houses for the dead and the pig-fat woman

The Flask
Pagan Practices

Many London pubs claim to be very old, but what is usually meant by this is that there has been a pub on the same site for a very long time; in fact, the vast majority of London's really old pubs were completely rebuilt in Victorian and Edwardian times, when no one could understand why anyone would want to preserve a crooked, low-ceilinged old tavern when they could have something grand and modern with high ceilings and big windows.

Here and there, however, a very old pub does survive, usually because it stayed in the same family for generations or perhaps because a particularly long-lived owner refused to have anything to do with ideas of redevelopment. One such example is The Flask in Hampstead. Renovated in the 1760s and again in 1910, it is still in essence a 17th-century tavern, once the haunt of highwaymen and footpads – including the infamous Dick Turpin (1706–39 – painters such as George Morland (1763–1804) and William Hogarth, and in slightly more recent times, Karl Marx (1818–83).

The Flask would originally have been a 'public

house of ill repute, a refuge for those of the lowest sort, outcasts and vagabonds', scorned by the well-to-do and on the edge of the dangerous, windswept and bandit-infested heath at Hampstead. Today, the low ceilings and ancient floorboards hint at this disreputable past, but if the highwaymen are gone the same cannot be said for one of London's most eccentric ceremonies, which is held here every year. This is the ceremony of Swearing on the Horns, which has a vague history but was certainly a feature of this part of north London in the 17th and 18th centuries. Lord Byron refers to it in his poem 'Childe Harold', and it seems to have all sorts of pagan associations. The ceremony died out at the end of the 19th century, but has recently been revived. It involves kissing a pair of antlers and promising to drink only good strong beer, and it is probably a debased, if fascinating, version of some ancient fertility rite.

At one time, as many as 20 Highgate and Hampstead pubs took part in the ritual twice a year. As each man kisses the antlers he has to promise to drink strong ale and no small beer; he is then given the freedom of Highgate, and may choose to kiss any girl who happens to be in the room at the time.

Highgate Cemetery
Dead Ahead

Highgate Cemetery is one of the strangest places in London. When it was opened in 1839, it became a fashionable place to meet and socialize as well as to be buried, and its 'residents' – as the dead were known – went to great lengths to ensure that their final resting places were architecturally perfect.

The grounds of the cemetery once belonged to a mansion owned by Sir William Ashurst, Mayor of London in 1693. The 20 acres (8 hectares) were landscaped at his expense by the garden architect David Ramsay, whose meandering lanes maximized the sense that this was a country park. These paths gradually work their way up to the highest ground in the cemetery, where a group of buildings and a terrace can be found next to the church of St Michael.

The buildings are approached via an Egyptian arch and avenue, lined with tombs. It is rather spooky today, particularly on a dark, wet afternoon, the whole edifice has an air of grandeur that seems out of place in a cemetery. At the end of the Egyptian Avenue is the Circle of Lebanon, surrounded by large, square architectural tombs rather like small houses. Each is fitted with niches for up to half a dozen family members. The tree in the middle of the circle dates back to the 17th century, when Sir William Ashurst walked here in the gardens of his house.

ABOVE: *Resembling something from an Ancient Greek or Roman city, the Circle of Lebanon in Highgate Cemetery provides a grand home for the wealthy dead.*

OPPOSITE: *The ancient ceremony of Swearing on the Horns is still practised in the Flask Inn in Hampstead.*

PREVIOUS PAGES: *The magnificent fireplace in the Old Queen's Head was reinstated after the original building was demolished in 1829.*

ABOVE: *In the days of coaches, the Assembly House was where jittery travellers would down some Dutch courage before taking the dangerous route to the north.*

From the time it was built right up to the present, Highgate Cemetery has attracted visitors. Originally they came to see the spectacular architectural edifices in which the dead were buried or to enjoy the view from this high point out across London. Now they come on organized tours – which are always a sell-out – to see the tombs of the great and the good: for here lie, among others too numerous to list, the novelist George Eliot (1819–80), the poet Christina Rossetti (1830–94), the scientist Michael Faraday (1791–1867) and, perhaps most famous of all, Karl Marx.

The Assembly House
Safety in Numbers

Crawling slowly up the hills of North London, early travellers in their cumbersome coaches were always vulnerable to attack by footpads and highwaymen.

One way to avoid them, or at least to reduce the chances of being robbed, was for travellers – both on foot and in their coaches – to get together before leaving. The greater the number in a travelling party, the safer they were likely to be.

And so a tradition grew up for travellers to gather at a spot on what is now Kentish Town Road. It was eminently sensible in the eyes of one early entrepreneur to build a tavern at this spot. The tavern is long gone, but another does stand on the site today, and is an extraordinary tribute to the palatial design instincts of Victorian architects.

In this great tradition of outrageous pub architecture, The Assembly House (as the pub has always been known) still has its extraordinary cut-glass mirrors and other elaborate decoration. It is a gin palace of spectacular dimensions. At a time when most of London's population lived in cramped, dark conditions, these light-filled halls with their lofty, elaborately decorated ceilings glittering with huge gas-powered lights must have been a tremendous draw – which was, of course, precisely what the builders intended.

Lady Lewson
Pig fat and rouge

Born around 1700, Mrs Lewson – or Lady Lewson as she became known – married a rich merchant at the age of 19 and moved to his house in Clerkenwell, then a quiet village on the edge of London.

Her husband died when she was only 26, but from that time until her death in about 1800 she rarely left the house. The beds in the house were always made, although no one ever came to stay. In over 60 years she never once cleaned the windows in the house, fearing they would be broken in the process or that the person cleaning them might be injured. And she refused to allow anything to be moved in any room, believing that to do so might cause her to catch cold.

In summer she was sometimes seen reading in her garden in attire that was far more appropriate to the fashion of about 1690, with 'ruffs and cuffs and fardingales', and she always wore her hair powdered and piled high on her head over a stiff horsehair frame. She believed that washing was highly dangerous and would lead to some 'dreadful disorder'; instead, she smeared her face and neck with pig fat, on top of which she applied a liberal quantity of pink powder.

Old Queen's Head
Soft Spot for the Ceiling

Islington has always been the place where many main routes from the North meet before the last short leg into the City. The junction at the Angel is one of the busiest in London, though hardly a trace remains of

ABOVE: *Lady Lewson believed that washing yourself was dangerous, and chose to cover herself in pig fat instead.*

the huge, creaking coaching inns that made the place famous before the coming of the railways.

The Angel Inn itself was the most famous, situated as it was almost on the junction where the road from the City met the roads from east and west, but despite its fame and former prosperity The Angel, and other old inns in the area, found themselves deserted by the 1840s. Trade had vanished, and they seemed like a relic – and not a very attractive one at that – of a less sophisticated age, so in the name of progress they were swept away. But one decidedly eccentric developer had a soft spot for The Old Queen's Head, which had existed for centuries on the Essex Road, a short distance from Islington Green. When it was demolished in 1829 he decided to put back some of what he had elsewhere taken out.

The Old Queen's Head, which was an early Tudor or Elizabethan building, had been almost as famous as The Angel itself. Sir Walter Raleigh (*c.* 1552–1618) certainly came here, as did Christopher Marlowe (1564–93) and other courtiers and wits of the 16th and 17th centuries. The front of the original pub had a sort of two-tiered gable, which was unique in the area, and inside it had ancient, elaborately decorated plaster ceilings and numerous dark-timbered, crooked bars with magnificent fireplaces. When the pub was demolished, one of the ceilings was taken out and reinstated in the new Victorian bar, together with one of the original fireplaces.

The most curious thing about these fragments of the past is that they were preserved at some cost at a time when the past was not seen as worth preserving at all. We owe it to the eccentricities of one builder that these wonderful relics have been preserved for us.

LEFT: *Fragments of the ancient Queen's Head, such as this splendid carving, were thankfully reinstalled by the Victorian redevelopers.*

OPPOSITE: *The New River flows peacefully through Islington, and few realize that it is the earliest surviving manmade attempt to bring fresh water to the City of London.*

New River
Water, Water Everywhere...

Along the backs of the houses in one or two streets in Canonbury, Islington, runs a narrow watercourse. To the casual observer it looks like an old canal, but closer inspection reveals something rather odd: this is far too narrow to be a canal, and yet neither is it a river or a stream. It is, in fact, a remnant of one of the earliest attempts to bring fresh water to London.

The New River Company started life in 1606, when acts of Parliament were passed to enable a channel to be dug to bring fresh water to central London from Amwell in Hertfordshire. Londoners were aware that it was unhealthy to throw all their rubbish and sewage into the same river (the Thames) from which they obtained their drinking water, but the practical difficulties involved in finding a water supply other than the Thames had always seemed insurmountable. The New River Company refused to accept defeat. Hugh Myddleton began the enormous task of digging a channel that was to be 10 feet wide by 4 feet deep (3 metres by 1 metre); its total length was a little under 40 miles (64km). All the work had to be done by hand, and much of it was carried out in the face of fierce opposition from landowners along the route. Myddleton ran out of money and had to be rescued by King James I, who offered financial assistance in return for a share of future profits.

By 1613 the route had been completed, and water ran into four newly built reservoirs at Clerkenwell. From here, water ran to the City through solid wooden pipes –which are still occasionally uncovered today during roadworks and building work. Though the system leaked badly, it was to provide water for many in the City for more than 200 years. The New River was adapted over the years, and its flow increased by additions from various newly dug wells and from the River Lea, but in essence it remained unchanged until 1904 when the New River Company was amalgamated with the Metropolitan Water Board. When the Second World War came to an end, a decision was made to stop using water from the remaining reservoirs at Clerkenwell, and though the flow continues to this day it now ends at Stoke Newington. A few stretches of the channel much closer to central London have survived, however, including that quiet backwater running through Canonbury.

Canonbury Tower
Roman Rubble

Although much of Islington succumbed to the dreaded 1960s town planners, it is also an area particularly rich in 18th- and 19th-century streets and squares. A few older gems survive, too, and among the strangest and most historic of these is Canonbury Tower.

At first glance this tall, square building might be 18th- or 19th-century, but look carefully at the base of the tower and it quickly becomes evident that this is a very ancient building indeed. Here the early rubble-and-brick courses appear to be Roman or older, and even above that early level the bricks have a mellow medieval look about them.

The name Canonbury comes from 'Canons Burgh' – because much of the land here, as well as the tower, was once owned by the canons of the great priory at Smithfield (whose church, St Bartholomew the Great, survives). The bulk of the surviving tower dates to the period just before the suppression of the monasteries in the mid-16th century: two rooms still have ceilings and fireplaces from the 1500s. The tower was, by this period, part of a manor house, and remnants of the rest of the house have also survived (two garden buildings can still be seen, for example), but when the priory at Smithfield was dissolved, the manor of Canonbury was given to Thomas Cromwell. He lost it when he lost his head and it passed to the Duke of Northumberland – who also lost his head! The house had a number of other owners, including a member of the Spencer family – whose wilful daughter Elizabeth is said to have been lowered from the top of the tower in a basket so that she could run off with the penniless

Lord Compton. The present Canonbury House (just round the corner from the tower) dates from the end of the 18th century. The tower is now part of a theatre and visitors are welcomed.

Kensal Green Cemetery
Grave Matters

Many visitors who include a cemetery on their London itinerary go to Highgate to the north of the City, but tucked away by the side of the Grand Union Canal over to the west, in what was until recently a fairly poor part of North Kensington, Kensal Green Cemetery is an extraordinary monument to Victorian funeral piety.

Until the arrival of the canal in the 18th century this was a quiet place: there were a few houses at the junction of Harrow Road and Kilburn Lane, but the rest was open farmland with the odd isolated inn and London a day's walk away. By the early 1800s, however, the small village centred on the junction and its green was expanding. At the same time, London's church graveyards were filled to bursting, and All Souls' Cemetery – as Kensal Green Cemetery was originally

ABOVE AND OPPOSITE: *The outlandish memorials at Kensal Green Cemetery reveal a great deal about the Victorian obsession with death.*

known (the land was owned by All Souls College, Oxford) – was opened in 1832 to ease the problem.

Within a few years Kensal Rise was *the* fashionable place to be buried, and it erupted with bizarre monuments – Greek temples, Egyptian halls, Gothic fantasies and miniature medieval castles – as well as more ordinary but equally fascinating gravestones and tombs. Look out for those of Sir Anthony Panizzi (1797–1879), who created the famous round reading room at the British Library (now part of the British Museum); Charles Babbage (1791–1871), who created the first computer; authors Wilkie Collins, William Makepeace Thackeray (1811–63) and Anthony Trollope (1815–82); and that great Victorian engineer, Isambard Kingdom Brunel (1806–59).

The cemetery is full of mature trees and shrubs, and gives every indication of being deep in the heart of the countryside. This is one of London's richest wildlife sites, with dozens of bird species, squirrels and foxes, butterflies and moths.

Contact Details

SOHO TO WESTMINSTER

Jeremy Bentham
South Cloisters,
University College
London (main
building),
Gower Street,
London WC1E 6BT
020 7679 2000
www.ucl.ac.uk

Berners Street
off Oxford Street,
London W1

Liberty Hall
Liberty, Regent Street,
London W1
020 7734 1234
www.liberty.co.uk

Café Royal
68 Regent Street,
London W1B 5EL
020 7437 9090

Burlington Arcade
Piccadilly,
London W1
www.burlington-
arcade.co.uk

Ritz Hotel
150 Piccadilly,
London W1J 9BR
020 7493 8181
www.theritzlondon.com

Fortnum and Mason
181 Piccadilly,
London W1A 1ER
020 7734 8040
www.fortnumand
mason.com

Albany
Piccadilly, London W1

Floris
89 Jermyn Street,
London SW1Y 6JH
0845 702 3239
www.florislondon.com

Eros
Trafalgar Square,
London WC2

Lock & Co. Hatters
6 St James's Street,
London SW1A 1EF
0 20 7930 8874
www.lockhatters.co.uk

Berry Bros & Rudd
3 St James's Street,
London SW1A 1EG
020 7396 9600
www.bbr.com

79 Pall Mall
London WC2

Duke of York's Column
Waterloo Place,
Carlton Terrace
(just off The Mall),
London SW1

Milkmaids in St James's
St James's Park,
London W1 1AA
020 7451 9999
www.innthepark.com

Craig's Court
just off Whitehall,
London SW1

Horse Guards
Whitehall,
London SW1

Henry VIII's Wine Cellar
Old War Office
Building, Whitehall,
London SW1A 2EU

Big Ben
Palace of Westminster,
London SW1A
020 7219 3000
www.parliament.uk

Westminster Hall
Palace of Westminster,
London SW1A
020 7219 3000
www.parliament.uk

Birdcage Walk
London SW1E

The Blewcoat School
23 Caxton Street,
Westminster,
London SW1H 0PY
020 7222 2877
www.nationaltrust.
org.uk

COVENT GARDEN

Seven Dials
Covent Garden,
London WC2

G. Smith & Sons
74 Charing Cross
Road, London
WC2H 0BG
020 7836 7422

Beefsteak Club
9 Irving Street
London WC2H

The Pearlies
www.pearlysociety.
co.uk

Trafalgar Square
London WC2

36 Craven Street
London WC2N 5NF
020 7930 9121

Gordon's Wine Bar
47 Villiers Street,
London WC2N 6NE
020 7930 1408

York Watergate
Victoria Embankment
Gardens, London
WC2

Cleopatra's Needle
Victoria Embankment,
London SW1

The Coal Hole
91 Strand, London
WC2R 0DW
020 7379 9883

The Savoy
1 Savoy Hill, London
WC2R 0BP
020 7950 5492
www.savoy-
group.co.uk

Rules
35 Maiden Lane,
Covent Garden,
London WC2E 7LB
020 7836 5314
www.rules.co.uk

Macklin Memorial
St Paul's Church,
Bedford Street,
Covent Garden,
London WC2E 9ED
020 7836.5221

HOLBORN & ST PAUL'S

Sir John Soane's Museum
13 Lincoln's Inn Fields,
London WC2A 3BP
020 7405 2107
www.soane.org

Prince Albert's Statue
Holborn Circus,
London EC1N

Weeping Monument
The Priory Church of
Saint Bartholomew
the Great, Cloth Fair,
London EC1A
020 7606 5171
www.greatstbarts.com

Ely Place
London EC1N

The Hand & Shears
1 Middle Street,
Cloth Fair,
London EC1A 7JA
020 7600 0257

John Donne's Monument, Amen Corner & Queen Anne's Statue
St Paul's Cathedral,
Ludgate Hill,
London EC4M
020 7236 4128
www.stpauls.co.uk

College of Arms
Queen Victoria Street,
London EC4V 4BT
020 7248 2762
www.college-of-
arms.gov.uk

Apothecaries Hall
Black Friars Lane,
London EC4V 6EJ
020 7236 1189
www.apothecaries.
org.uk

The Black Friar
174 Queen Victoria
Street, London
EC4V 4EG
020 7236 5650

St Bride's Church
Fleet Street,
London EC4Y 8AU
020 7427 0133
www.stbrides.com

Salisbury Square
London EC4

Ye Olde Cheshire Cheese
145 Fleet Street,
London EC4A 2BU
020 7353 6170

Dr Johnson's House
17 Gough Square,
London EC4A 3DE
020 7353 3745
www.drjh.dircon.co.uk

Prince Henry's Room
17 Fleet Street,
London EC4Y 1AA
020 7936 4004

Ede and Ravenscroft
2 Gracechurch Street,
London EC3V 0DD
020 7929 1848

Law Courts' Clock
Law Courts, Strand,
London WC2

Twinings Tea Shop
216 The Strand,
London WC2R 1AP
020 7353 3511
www.twinings.co.uk

Coutts Bank
440 Strand, London
WC2R 0QS
020 7753 1000
www.coutts.com

Kingsway Tram Slope
Embankment,
London WC2

Somerset House
Strand, London
WC2R 1LA
020 7845 4600
www.somerset-
house.org.uk

Strand Roman Bath
5 Strand Lane,
London WC2R 2NA
www.nationaltrust.
org.uk

No. 2 Temple Place
London WC2R 3BD
020 7836 3715
www.twotempleplace.
co.uk

Embankment Lions
Embankment,
London WC2

WEST & SOUTH-WEST LONDON
Dog Cemetery
Hyde Park,
London W2 2UH
020 7298 2000
www.royalparks.gov.uk

15 South Street
London W1

**The Eccentric
Fisherman**
The Serpentine,
Hyde Park,
London W2 2UH
020 7298 2000

Wellington Arch
Apsley Way,
Hyde Park Corner,
London SW1X 7LY
020 7930 2726

**Linley Sambourne
House**
18 Stafford Terrace,
London W8
020 7602 3316
www.rbkc.gov.uk/lin-
leysambournehouse

Leighton House
12 Holland Park Road,
London W14 8LZ
020 7602 3316
www.rbkc.gov.uk/Leig
htonHouseMuseum

Carlyle's House
24 Cheyne Row,
Chelsea, London
SW3 5HL
020 7352 7087
www.nationaltrust.org.
uk

Albert Bridge
Chelsea,
London SW3

Crosby Hall
Cheyne Walk,
Chelsea,
London SW3

Japanese Peace Pagoda
Battersea Park,
London SW11
020 7228 9620
www.batterseapark.org

Crapper & Co.
120 King's Road,
Chelsea,
London SW3
www.thomas-
crapper.com

Sloane Square Station
Sloane Square,
London SW1W 8BB
www.tfl.gov.uk

Fulham Bottle Kiln
New King's Road,
Fulham, London SW6

**London Wetland
Centre**
The Wildfowl &
Wetlands Trust,
Queen Elizabeth's
Walk, Barnes,
London SW13 9WT
020 8409 4400
www.wwt.org.uk/visit/
wetlandcentre

SOUTH & SOUTH-EAST LONDON
Bedlam in Lambeth
Lambeth Road,
London SE1 6HZ
020 7416 5000
www.iwm.org.uk

Saatchi Gallery
County Hall,
South Bank,
London SE1 7PB
020 7823 2363
www.saatchi-
gallery.co.uk

Oxo Tower
Oxo Tower Wharf,
Bargehouse Street,
South Bank, London
SE1 9PH
020 7401 2255
www.oxotower.co.uk

Cardinal's Wharf
Bankside, London SE1

Anchor Inn
234 Park Street,
Bankside, London
SE1 9EF
020 7407 1577
www.fatbadgers.co.uk

John Elwes
Southwark Cathedral,
London Bridge,
London SE1 9DA
020 7367 6700

The George Inn
The George Inn Yard,
77 Borough High
Street, Southwark
London SE1 1NH

020 7407 2056
www.nationaltrust.
org.uk

Rotherhithe
London SE16
www.rotherhithe.
org.uk

Brixton Windmill
Windmill Gardens,
Blenheim Gardens,
Brixton, London SW2
020 7926 1052

**Crystal Palace
Dinosaurs**
Crystal Palace Park,
Thicket Road, Penge,
London SE20 8DT
020 8778 9496

EAST LONDON
Bunhill Fields
Bunhill Row,
London EC1Y 8LP

Dirty Dicks
202 Bishopsgate,
London EC2M 4NR
020 7283 5888

Artillery Lane
London E1

Aldgate Pump
Aldgate High Street,
London EC3

Hoop & Grapes
47 Aldgate High
Street, London
EC3N 1AL
020 7265 5171

The Geffrye Museum
Kingsland Road,
London E2 8EA
020 7739 9893
www.geffrye-
museum.org.uk

**Museum of
Childhood**
Cambridge Heath
Road
London E2 9PA
020 8980 2415
www.vam.ac.uk/
vastatic/nmc/

Sutton House
2 & 4 Homerton High
Street, Hackney,
London E9 6JQ
020 8986 2264
www.nationaltrust.org.
uk

**Abbey Mills Pumping
Station**
Stratford, London E15

River Lea
Stratford, London E15

NORTH LONDON
The Flask
14 Flask Walk,
Hampstead,
London NW3 1HE
020 7435 4580

Highgate Cemetery
Swain's Lane,
Highgate, London
N6 6PJ
020 8340 1834
http://highgate-
cemetery.org

The Assembly House
292–294 Kentish
Town Road, London
NW5 2TG
020 7485 2031

Old Queen's Head
4 Essex Road, London
N1 8LN
020 7354 9273

New River
Islington, London N1

Canonbury Tower
Canonbury Place,
Islington, London
N1 2NQ
020 7359 6888

**Kensal Green
Cemetery**
Harrow Road,
Kensal Green,
London W10 4RA
www.kensalgreen.co.uk

Index

Picture Acknowledgements

Page 8 (right): Narcissus Hall, Leighton House, London (photo), Leighton House Museum and Art Gallery, London, UK/ www.bridgeman.co.uk
Page 12: Courtesy of University College London Special Collections
Page 14: Courtesy of Red or Dead
Page 27 (left): Mary Evans Picture Library
Page 30: Mary Evans Picture Library
Page 31: Time Life Pictures/Getty Images
Page 33: Deryc R. Sands, Palace of Westminster
Page 34: Mary Evans Picture Library
Page 48: Courtesy of The Savoy
Page 52: By courtesy of the Trustees of Sir John Soane's Museum. Photo: Martin Charles.
Page 55: Chris Coe
Page 61: Chris Coe

Page 63 (bottom): Mary Evans Picture Library
Page 70: Courtesy of Coutts & Co.
Page 71: Mary Evans Picture Library
Page 76: PA Photos Ltd
Page 81: The Drawing Room (photo), Linley Sambourne House, London, UK/www.bridgeman.co.uk
Page 83: Detail of the Arab Hall, 1870s (photo) by George II Aitchison (1825–1910), Leighton House Museum and Art Gallery, London, UK/www.bridgeman.co.uk
Page 87: Courtesy of Thomas Crapper & Company, Ltd
Page 92: Mary Evans Picture Library
Page 108: Courtesy of Guildhall Library, London
Page 113: Gilly Cameron Cooper:
Page 118: Eric Nathan
Page 119: Mary Evans Picture Library